제6판

교원임용고시
일반영어 필독서

임용영어 수험생 대다수가 선택하는
전공영어의 보통명사

- 교원임용고시 전공영어 독보적 전국 1위
  (2025년 예스24 전공영어 부문 박문각 누적 판매량 1위)
- 미국 버클리대학 유희태 박사의 일반영어 필독서
- 2S2R 원리를 유형에 구체적 적용

유희태 일반영어

2S2R ❷ 유형

LSI 영어연구소 유희태 박사 저

PREFACE

2026년 《2S2R 유형》 6판을 내며

《2S2R 유형》은 2014년 초판이 출간된 후, 1년 후인 2015년에 개정판, 2017년에 3판, 2020년에 4판, 2022년에 5판이 차례로 나왔다. 그러나 4판과 5판은 내용뿐 아니라 형식면에서도 큰 변화가 없었기에, 이번 6판은 6년 만에 선보이는 완전 개정판이라 할 수 있다. 이번 6판은 5판이 가지고 있는 여러 한계를 극복하기 위해 새롭게 출간되었다.

이 6판 교재는 특히 형식적인 측면에서, 그동안 챕터별로 세분화되어 있던 요지, 목적, 제목, 지칭추론 등 다양한 영역을 압축 및 정리하여 간결하게 구성했다. 이는 최근 임용시험에서 해당 영역들을 이전만큼 비중 있게 다루지 않기 때문이다. 또한 '2S2R 방법론의 구체화'라는 지향점을 가진 《2S2R 유형》 교재의 철학을 한층 더 밀도 있게 구현했다. 즉, 《2S2R 기본》에서 배운 2S2R 방법론을 심화할 수 있도록 교재를 정교화했으며, 동시에 내용의 양도 대폭 확대했다.

《유희태 일반영어 시리즈 ② - 2S2R 유형》은 《유희태 일반영어 시리즈 ① - 2S2R 기본》, 《유희태 일반영어 시리즈 ③ - 2S2R 기출》, 《유희태 일반영어 시리즈 ④ - 1 - 2S2R 문제은행》, 《유희태 일반영어 시리즈 ④ - 2 - 2S2R 문제은행》, 《유희태 일반영어 시리즈 ⑤ - 기출 VOCA 30days》의 자매편이다. 모든 시리즈를 체계적으로 공부한다면 점수가 잘 오르지 않는 일반영어 과목에서 목적한 바의 성취를 충분히 얻을 것이다.

『유희태 2S2R 시리즈』를 효과적으로 활용하는 방법은, 대학 1학년 때 《2S2R 기본》을 최소 3회독, 평균 5회독하여 일반영어 기본이론을 확실하게 다진 뒤, 2학년 때 《2S2R 유형》을 최소 3회독하여 임용 유형에 기본이론을 확장 적용하는 훈련을 하고, 3학년 때 《2S2R 기출》을 2회독한 다음, 처음으로 임용시험을 치르는 4학년 때 《2S2R 문제은행》을 가지고 공부하는 것이다. 이 과정에서 《기출 VOCA 30days》는 1학년 때부터 주 6회 매일 20분씩 꾸준히 공부하기를 추천한다. 그러면 4학년 11월 임용시험을 치를 때가 되면, 임용에 필요한 어휘의 80%는 머릿속에 차곡차곡 쌓여서, 독해를 하는 데 있어 어휘의 부족은 느끼지 않을 것이다.

이 6판 작업을 하면서 많은 분들의 도움을 받았다. 원고를 보기 좋은 최종 결과물로 만들어준 박문각의 변수경 편집자와 박용 회장님께 고마움을 전한다. 또한 교재가 세상에 나오기까지 묵묵히 최선을 다해주신 모든 인쇄·출판 노동자분들께도 깊은 감사의 마음을 전한다. 아무쪼록 이 《2S2R 유형》 6판 교재가 수험생 여러분의 합격에 일조하기를 깊은 마음으로 바란다.

2026년 새해를 앞두고 LSI 영어연구소에서

유희태

CONTENTS

PART 01 기입형

빈칸추론 ··· 8

PART 02 서술형

A형 서술형 ··· 60

B형 서술형 ··· 190

2S2R

유희태 일반영어
② 유형

PART 01
기입형

01 Read the passage and follow the directions. [2 points]

The concept of two warring souls within the body of the Black American was as meaningful for Du Bois at the end of his years as editor of *Crisis*, the official journal of the National Association for the Advancement of Colored People (NAACP), as when he had first used the image at the start of the century. The tension between race pride and identification with the nation as a whole was nowhere more dramatic than in the most controversial editorial ever printed in *Crisis*, "Close Ranks," which in July 1918 called on Black Americans to "forget our special grievances and close our ranks" with the White people "fighting for democracy" during the First World War. Bitterly criticized by Black people, Du Bois barely modified his statement when, two months later, he set the priorities for his readers: "first your Country, then your Rights!" Perhaps the editor had written more than he intended in using the word "forget," for *Crisis* before and after the editorial showed no diminution in its criticism of racism. But he distinguished between Allied and German ambitions, and declared that defeat of the former would be disastrous for that "United States of the World" to which he was most loyal. Du Bois nevertheless saw danger in the negation of race pride, by those who did not recognize their own beauty as Black people, for example. The responsibility of *Crisis* was to arbitrate between those who advocated _____ and those who denied any differences between the races. The focal point of the magazine's efforts in this respect came with the rise of Marcus Garvey, the gifted Jamaican leader whose "back-to-Africa" movement, as it was popularly called, was founded on the premise, according to Du Bois, that "a black skin was in itself a sort of patent to nobility."

Fill in the blank with the TWO most appropriate consecutive words from the passage.

_____

_____

NOTE

Step 1	**S**urvey
Key Words	
Signal Words	
Step 2	**R**eading
Purpose	
Pattern of Organization	
Tone	
Main Idea	
Step 3	**S**ummary
지문 요약하기 (Paraphrasing)	
Step 4	**R**ecite
요약문 말로 설명하기	

02 **Read the passage and follow the directions.** [2 points]

> The celebrated philosopher William James proposed a distinction between voluntary and involuntary attention. When you cross a busy intersection, you are depleting finite reserves of voluntary, directed attention. The antidote is not to sit quietly in a darkened room. The environment has to have some kind of stimulation to activate your involuntary attention—your fascination. Urban environments can clearly elicit involuntary attention (honking horns in Times Square), but they do so in a harsh, peremptory way that requires voluntary attention to override. Natural environments, on the other hand, provide softly fascinating stimulation. Your eye is captured by the shape of a branch, a ripple in the water; your mind follows.
>
> An eminent scholar conducted a study in which he sent volunteers on a fifty-minute walk through either an arboretum or city streets, then gave his subjects a cognitive assessment. Those who had taken the nature walk performed about twenty per cent better than their counterparts on tests of memory and attention. They also tended to be in a better mood, although that didn't affect their scores. However, people don't have to like the interaction with nature to get the benefits. Some of the walks took place in June, whereas others took place in January; most people didn't particularly enjoy trudging through the harsh Michigan winter, but their scores jumped just as much as in the summer trials. Not surprisingly, those whose directed _____ is most depleted seem to get the biggest benefits: an end-of-workday nature romp packs a greater restorative punch than one first thing in the morning, and the boost is five times bigger in people who have been diagnosed with clinical depression.

Fill in the blank with the ONE most appropriate word from the passage.

NOTE

Step 1	**S**urvey
Key Words	
Signal Words	
Step 2	**R**eading
Purpose	
Pattern of Organization	
Tone	
Main Idea	
Step 3	**S**ummary
지문 요약하기 (Paraphrasing)	
Step 4	**R**ecite
	요약문 말로 설명하기

03 Read the passage and follow the directions. [2 points]

The diminution of individual liberty is likely to continue, since it has two continuing causes. On the one hand, modern technique makes society more organic; on the other hand, modern sociology makes men more and more aware of the causal laws in virtue of which one man's acts are useful or harmful to another man. If we are to justify any particular form of individual liberty in the scientific society of the future, we shall have to do it on the ground that that form of liberty is for the utility of society as a whole, but not in most cases on the ground that the acts concerned affect nobody but the agent.

Let us take some examples of traditional principles which appear no longer defensible. The first example that occurs to me is as regards the investment of capital. At present, within wide limits, any man who has money to invest may invest it as he chooses. This freedom was defended during the heyday of laissezfaire on the ground that the business which paid best was always the most socially useful. Few men nowadays would dare to maintain such a doctrine. Nevertheless the old freedom persists. It is clear that in a scientific society capital would be invested where its social _____ is greatest, not where it earns the highest rate of profits. The rate of profits earned depends often upon quite accidental circumstances.

Fill in the blank with the ONE most appropriate word from the passage.

NOTE

Step 1	**S**urvey
Key Words	
Signal Words	

Step 2	**R**eading
Purpose	
Pattern of Organization	
Tone	
Main Idea	

Step 3	**S**ummary
지문 요약하기 (Paraphrasing)	

Step 4	**R**ecite
	요약문 말로 설명하기

04 Read the passage and follow the directions. [2 points]

> Cannabis is a popular recreational drug and its legal status has been a source of enduring controversy. In a recent study, David Pagliaccio, Ph.D. and coauthors analyzed data from a group of twin/siblings to determine whether cannabis use was associated with brain volumes. To determine whether any significant differences could be attributed to predispositional /familial or causal factors, brain volumes were compared across twin/sibling pairs. Among 241 twin/sibling pairs, 89 pairs were discordant for cannabis exposure, 81 pairs were concordant for cannabis exposure and 71 pairs were concordantly unexposed to cannabis. Among all 482 study participants, cannabis exposure was related to smaller left amygdala and right ventral striatum volumes. Volume differences were in the range of normal variation.
>
> However, brain volumes did not differ between siblings discordant for cannabis exposure. Both the exposed and unexposed siblings in pairs discordant for cannabis exposure showed smaller amygdala volumes relative to _____ unexposed pairs. "When using a simple index of exposure (i.e. ever vs. never use), we found no evidence for the causal influence of cannabis exposure on amygdala volume. Future work characterizing the roles of causal and predispositional factors underpinning neural changes at various degrees of cannabis involvement may provide targets for substance abuse policy and prevention programs," the authors conclude.

Fill in the blank with the ONE most appropriate word from the passage.

_____

_____

NOTE

Step 1	**S**urvey
Key Words	
Signal Words	
Step 2	**R**eading
Purpose	
Pattern of Organization	
Tone	
Main Idea	
Step 3	**S**ummary
지문 요약하기 (Paraphrasing)	
Step 4	**R**ecite
	요약문 말로 설명하기

05 Read the passage and follow the directions. [2 points]

> In suggesting any curtailment of liberty there are always two quite distinct questions to be considered. The first is whether such a curtailment would be in the public interest if it were wisely carried out, and the second is whether it will be in the public interest when it is carried out with a certain measure of ignorance and perversity. These two questions are in theory quite distinct, but from the point of view of the government the second question does not exist, since every government believes itself entirely free from both ignorance and perversity. Every government, consequently, in so far as it is not restrained by traditional prejudices, will advocate more interference with liberty than is wise. When, therefore, we are considering what interferences with liberty might be theoretically justified, we must hesitate to draw the conclusion that they should be advocated in practice. I think it probable, however, that almost all interferences with liberty for which there is a theoretical justification will, in time, be carried out in practice, because scientific technique is gradually making governments so strong that they need not consider outside opinion. The result of this will be that governments will be able to interfere with individual liberty wherever in their opinion there is a sound reason for so doing, and for the reason just given, this will be much more often than it should be. For this reason _____ is likely to lead to a governmental tyranny which may in time prove disastrous.

Fill in the blank with the TWO most appropriate consecutive words from the passage.

_____

_____

N.O.T.E

Step 1	Survey
Key Words	
Signal Words	
Step 2	**Reading**
Purpose	
Pattern of Organization	
Tone	
Main Idea	
Step 3	**Summary**
지문 요약하기 (Paraphrasing)	
Step 4	**Recite**
	요약문 말로 설명하기

06 Read the passage and follow the directions. [2 points]

> Pidgins and creoles are the outcome of the need of people not sharing a language to communicate but differ from national and international languages in that a pidgin does not begin as an already existing language or dialect selected to serve this purpose; it is rather a particular combination of two languages.
>
> A pidgin is a marginal language which arises to fulfill certain restricted communication needs among people who have no common language. In the initial stages of contact the ____ⓐ____ is often limited to transactions where a detailed exchanged of ideas is not required and where a small vocabulary, drawn almost exclusively from one language, suffices. The syntactic structure of the pidgin is less complex and less flexible than the structures of the languages that were in contact, and though many pidgin features clearly reflect usages in the contact languages others are unique to the pidgin.
>
> A creole arises when a pidgin becomes the mother tongue of a speech community. The simple structure that characterized the pidgin is carried over into the creole but since a creole, as a mother tongue, must be capable of expressing the whole range of human experience, the lexicon is expanded, and frequently a more elaborate syntactic system evolves. Since creoles are often not regarded as "real" languages and consequently considered as inferior, it is worth noting that, for example, both French and English may be the outcome of pidgins—in the first case through ____ⓑ____ between native Gauls and occupying Romans, and in the second through ____ⓑ____ between the native Anglo-Saxons and the Danes who settled on the east coast of England.

Fill in each blank ⓐ and ⓑ with the ONE most appropriate word from the passage respectively.

_____

_____

NOTE

Step 1	**S**urvey
Key Words	
Signal Words	
Step 2	**R**eading
Purpose	
Pattern of Organization	
Tone	
Main Idea	
Step 3	**S**ummary
지문 요약하기 (Paraphrasing)	
Step 4	**R**ecite
	요약문 말로 설명하기

07 Read the passage and follow the directions. [2 points]

> Electricity, like light, travels extremely fast, at 300,000 kilometers per second. It flows easily through metal wires. In particular, copper and silver are very good conductors of electricity. Electricity also generates heat as it flows through most objects. It can be controlled and utilized easily using many different technologies. Electricity is very useful because it can be converted into many kinds of ____①____. Electricity can be converted in to light using light bulbs, and even heat by using heating coils. It can also be converted into motion or even stored chemical energy. Electricity is used everywhere; to produce goods, provide services, and transport materials and people. Electricity also is used in commerce, agriculture, medicine, communications, entertainment, and a variety of other areas. Expanded uses for electricity are constantly being developed. Not only does electricity provide energy it also provides ____②____. A total of 510,595 workers were employed by electric utilities at the end of 1990 in a wide variety of jobs. From repairing power lines, to providing information to electricity customers, to constructing new power plants.

Fill in each blank with the ONE most appropriate word from the passage respectively.

_____

_____

NOTE

Step 1	**S**urvey
Key Words	
Signal Words	
Step 2	**R**eading
Purpose	
Pattern of Organization	
Tone	
Main Idea	
Step 3	**S**ummary
지문 요약하기 (Paraphrasing)	
Step 4	**R**ecite
	요약문 말로 설명하기

08 Read the passage and follow the directions. [2 points]

> One of the things is you have to be able to find a really interesting problem that is soluble, that you don't have to wait for exploration to Jupiter to solve, and yet is an important problem. They're not in Antarctica or on Mars. They're right around us in the air. I heard a wonderful talk in this very building about black holes. There may be billions of microscopic black holes in every room in Dwinelle. It was a brilliant talk. You can see that what we don't know is right around us. Somebody once said if the fish were going to study the world, the last thing they would discover would be the ocean. Because we're so immersed in everyday things. A scientist is very different than a scientific worker. Most of the people that society calls "scientists" are what I call "scientific workers." A scientist is very much like a(n) _____. You do your best work lying awake in the afternoon. You have dreams and you have random thoughts and you have motivations that you don't understand, and stray bits of information that you put together from different sources, and you get an idea. And this idea is like a poem. John Keats, who was a doctor as well as a poet, just would suddenly—some beautiful lines of poetry would come into his head. I think that's the way real scientists work.

Fill in the blank with the ONE most appropriate word from the passage.

NOTE

Step 1	**S**urvey
Key Words	
Signal Words	
Step 2	**R**eading
Purpose	
Pattern of Organization	
Tone	
Main Idea	
Step 3	**S**ummary
지문 요약하기 (Paraphrasing)	
Step 4	**R**ecite
	요약문 말로 설명하기

09 Read the passage and follow the directions. [2 points]

The early twentieth century marked a period of rapid industrial and technological change in a society which began to redefine the roles of the individual and society. Max Weber and Sigmund Freud were two revolutionary thinkers of the time who recognized the importance of this relationship and tried to determine whether the power balance between society and the individual was tilted in one particular direction or the other. A world becoming an increasingly complex and restrictive forced these thinkers to ask themselves if society had indeed finally become a force too dynamic for the individual to manipulate; that if in fact it was society that had mastered the man. Although both thinkers provide radically different views of culture and society they are both essentially trying to answer the same question: does the individual control society or does society control the individual?

The relevance of such an argument might first be debated, for one might first respond to this question with some doubt; surely we have control of ourselves, do we all not have control of our own faculties at this very moment? At this moment you are reading or being subjected to a reading of this paper, therefore if this indeed is not fulfilling some immediate obvious desire it is accomplishing some sort of other goal. Likely this goal is to achieve an education but again we might ask ourselves why? Surely we all want to further our scholarly qualities and develop our minds but more likely this again has an underlying goal: to _____ in society. Society has shown us that in most cases it requires a good deal of education in order to succeed. Therefore we might entertain the question, is our presence here a product of our own desires or that of society's? The point of this reasoning is only to point out something we may not immediately recognize: regardless of what our own free will may dictate, we cannot help but be influenced by the values and morals of modern-day society.

Fill in the blank with the ONE most appropriate word from the passage.

_____

_____

NOTE

Step 1	**S**urvey
Key Words	
Signal Words	
Step 2	**R**eading
Purpose	
Pattern of Organization	
Tone	
Main Idea	
Step 3	**S**ummary
지문 요약하기 (Paraphrasing)	
Step 4	**R**ecite
	요약문 말로 설명하기

10 Read the passage and follow the directions. [2 points]

> Fatigue is of many sorts, some of which are a much graver obstacle to happiness than others. Purely ___ⓐ___, provided it is not excessive, tends if anything to be a cause of happiness; it leads to sound sleep and a good appetite, and gives zest to the pleasures that are possible on holidays. But when it is excessive it becomes a very grave evil. Peasant women in all but the most advanced communities are old at thirty, worn out with excessive toil. Children in the early days of industrialism were stunted in their growth and frequently killed by overwork in early years. The same thing still happens in China and Japan, where industrialism is new; to some extent also in the Southern States of America. Physical labour carried beyond a certain point is atrocious torture, and it has very frequently been carried so far as to make life all but unbearable. In the most advanced parts of the modern world, however, physical fatigue has been much minimized through the improvement of industrial conditions. The kind of fatigue that is most serious in the present day in advanced communities is ___ⓑ___. This kind, oddly enough, is most pronounced among the well-to-do, and tends to be much less among wage-earners than it is among business men and brain-workers. To escape from nervous fatigue in modern life is a very difficult thing.

Fill in each blank with the TWO most appropriate consecutive words from the passage respectively.

_____

_____

NOTE

Step 1	**S**urvey
Key Words	
Signal Words	
Step 2	**R**eading
Purpose	
Pattern of Organization	
Tone	
Main Idea	
Step 3	**S**ummary
지문 요약하기 (Paraphrasing)	
Step 4	**R**ecite
	요약문 말로 설명하기

11 Read the passage and follow the directions. [2 points]

> The race to the bottom is a socioeconomic concept that occurs between nations. When competition becomes fierce between nations over a particular area of trade and production, the nations are given increased incentive to dismantle currently existing regulatory standards. It may be seen that with the global push towards free trade, labor is now very susceptible to the race to the bottom model. With an extremely large labor pool to draw from worldwide and a virtually unrestricted ability to move capital, multi-national corporations may now freely move their operations from country to country, following the most affordable labor. This in turn affects labor laws, particularly in developing countries, where things such as minimum wage or required overtime pay create a large barrier to lowest-cost labor. The _____, therefore, dictates that more and more nations (again, particularly in the developing world) will eliminate their labor laws.

Fill in the blank with the most appropriate consecutive words from the passage.

_____
_____

NOTE

Step 1	**S**urvey
Key Words	
Signal Words	
Step 2	**R**eading
Purpose	
Pattern of Organization	
Tone	
Main Idea	
Step 3	**S**ummary
지문 요약하기 (Paraphrasing)	
Step 4	**R**ecite
	요약문 말로 설명하기

12 Read the passage and follow the directions. [2 points]

When we know the initial conditions of an orderly system, we can make predictions about it. For example, in the Newtonian macroworld, knowing with precision the initial conditions lets us state where a planet will be after a certain time, where a launched rocket will land, and when an eclipse will occur. Similarly, in the quantum microworld we can predict where an electron is likely to be in an atom, and the probability that a radioactive particle will decay in a given time interval. Predictability in orderly systems, both Newtonian and quantum, depends on knowledge of initial conditions. Some systems, however, whether Newtonian or quantum, are not orderly—they are inherently ___①___. These are called "chaotic systems." Turbulent water flow is an example. No matter how precisely we know the initial conditions of a piece of floating wood as it flows downstream, we cannot predict its location later downstream. A feature of chaotic systems is that slight differences in initial conditions result in wildly different outcomes later. Two identical pieces of wood just slightly apart at one time are vastly far apart soon thereafter. Weather is ___②___. Small changes in one day's weather can produce big (and largely unpredictable) changes a week later. Meteorologists try their best, but they are bucking the hard fact of chaos in nature. This barrier to good prediction first led the scientist Edward Lorenz to ask, "Does the flap of a butterfly's wings in Brazil set off a tornado in Texas?" Now we talk about the "butterfly effect" when we are dealing with situations where very small effects can amplify into very big effects.

Fill in each blank with the ONE most appropriate word from the passage respectively.

_____

_____

NOTE

Step 1	Survey
Key Words	
Signal Words	
Step 2	**Reading**
Purpose	
Pattern of Organization	
Tone	
Main Idea	
Step 3	**Summary**
지문 요약하기 (Paraphrasing)	
Step 4	**Recite**
	요약문 말로 설명하기

13 Read the passage and follow the directions. [2 points]

> Observation depends on ____①____ and knowledge. If three friends travel abroad, one an architect, another a botanist, and the third a stockbroker, then the architect is likely to notice the style of houses and other buildings more than his friends do, because he is specially interested in them. The botanist will observe especially the flowers and trees of the country more than his friends; and s/he will actually see more details because s/he knows what to look for. Observation is guided by knowledge and prompted by interest. We have, however, no reason to suppose that the botanist, trained in such observation, or the architect, keenly observant of the buildings, will be more observant than the stockbroker of the faces of the foreign people they meet, or the dress of the women. Indeed, they are more likely to have their attention diverted by the objects of their special interests. So training in the careful ____②____ of the varied endings of Latin words, or of the changes in chemical substances in experiments, will have no effect on the observation of pictures or the movement of stars.

Fill in each blank with the ONE most appropriate word from the passage.

_____

_____

NOTE

Step 1	**S**urvey
Key Words	
Signal Words	
Step 2	**R**eading
Purpose	
Pattern of Organization	
Tone	
Main Idea	
Step 3	**S**ummary
지문 요약하기 (Paraphrasing)	
Step 4	**R**ecite
	요약문 말로 설명하기

14 Read the passage and follow the directions. [2 points]

> The concept of sustainability applies to all aspects of life on Earth and is commonly defined within ____①____, social and economic contexts. Due to factors such as overpopulation, lack of education, inadequate financial circumstances and the actions of past generations, sustainability can be difficult to achieve. In an ecological context, sustainability is defined as the ability of an ecosystem to maintain ecological processes, functions, biodiversity and productivity into the future. In a social context, sustainability is expressed as meeting the needs of the present without compromising the ability of future generations to meet their own needs. When applied in an economic context, a business is sustainable if it has adapted its practices for the use of renewable resources and is accountable for the environmental impacts of its activities. To be sustainable, regardless of context, Earth's resources must be used at a rate at which they can be replenished. There is now clear scientific evidence that humanity is living unsustainably, and that an effort is needed to keep human use of Earth's resources within ____②____ limits.

Fill in each blank with the ONE most appropriate word from the passage.

_____

_____

NOTE

Step 1	**S**urvey
Key Words	
Signal Words	
Step 2	**R**eading
Purpose	
Pattern of Organization	
Tone	
Main Idea	
Step 3	**S**ummary
지문 요약하기 (Paraphrasing)	
Step 4	**R**ecite
	요약문 말로 설명하기

15 Read the passage and follow the directions. [2 points]

> In the early factories the employers went so far as to manipulate their clocks or sound their factory whistles at the wrong times in order to cheat the workers out of a little of this valuable new commodity. Later such practices became less frequent, but the influence of the clock imposed regularity on the lives of the majority of men that had previously been known only in the monasteries. Men actually became like clocks, acting with a repetitive ____①____ which had no resemblance to the rhythmic life of a natural being. They became, as the Victorian phrase put it, "as regular as clockwork." Only in the country districts where the natural lives of animals and plants and the elements still dominated existence, did any large proportion of the population fail to yield to the deadly tick of monotony.
>
> At first this new attitude to time, this new regularity of life, was imposed by the clock-owning masters on the unwilling poor. The factory slave reacted in his spare time by living with a chaotic irregularity which characterized the slums of early nineteenth-century industrialism. Men fled to the timeless worlds of drink or Methodist inspiration. But gradually the idea of regularity spread downwards and among the workers. Nineteenth-century religion and morality played their part by proclaiming the sin of "wasting time." The introduction of mass-produced watches and clocks in the 1850s spread time-consciousness among those who had previously merely reacted to the stimulus of the knocker-up or the factory whistle. In the church and the school, in the office and the workshop, ____②____ was held up as the greatest of the virtues.

Fill in each blank ① and ② respectively with the ONE most appropriate word from the passage.

NOTE

Step 1	**S**urvey
Key Words	
Signal Words	
Step 2	**R**eading
Purpose	
Pattern of Organization	
Tone	
Main Idea	
Step 3	**S**ummary
지문 요약하기 (Paraphrasing)	
Step 4	**R**ecite
	요약문 말로 설명하기

16 Read the passage and follow the directions. [2 points]

> Standardized entrance exams have played a major role in the college admissions process since the late 1920s, and their significance has grown over the past several decades. The prominence of these tests, however, has been coupled with controversy about their fairness and effectiveness in determining college success. College entrance exams, in particular the SAT, have been targets of criticism for years. Critics claim that the exams are biased against minorities, women and low-income students; lack fairness in how they sort students; and contribute to an overly competitive admissions process. Futhermore, students are under pressure to increase their scores for admissions and financial aid purposes; teachers are under pressure to help students score well; and colleges and universities are under pressure to admit students with high scores to improve their rankings and fundraising abilities. Detractors have long argued that far too much emphasis is placed on _____ for college admissions that, in their opinion, do not accurately reflect the range of student talents or their commitment to succeed at the postsecondary level.

Fill in the blank with the TWO most appropriate consecutive words from the passage.

_____

_____

NOTE

Step 1	**S**urvey
Key Words	
Signal Words	
Step 2	**R**eading
Purpose	
Pattern of Organization	
Tone	
Main Idea	
Step 3	**S**ummary
지문 요약하기 (Paraphrasing)	
Step 4	**R**ecite
	요약문 말로 설명하기

17 Read the passage and follow the directions. [2 points]

> Throughout human history, men have been generally engaged in social life such as laboring for money and food and public gathering for power; hence, men have looked for ____①____. On the other hand, it has been women who acquired their happiness by bearing and rearing children. In women's view, public accomplishment makes a man attractive and desirable as a marriage partner or a father of future children. But for men, the condition is the opposite. The more a woman tries to accomplish socially, the less charming and desirable she seems to a man as a wife. This gender bias, however, does not appear to be quite evidenced, especially in the modern societies in terms of economic and technical development, due to the fact that more women prefer to have jobs than to raise children and that more ____②____ seem to be settled in the house to run household affairs.

Fill in the blank ① with the TWO most appropriate consecutive words from the passage. Then fill in the blank ② with the ONE most appropriate word from the passage.

Step 1	**S**urvey
Key Words	
Signal Words	
Step 2	**R**eading
Purpose	
Pattern of Organization	
Tone	
Main Idea	
Step 3	**S**ummary
지문 요약하기 (Paraphrasing)	
Step 4	**R**ecite
	요약문 말로 설명하기

18 Read the passage and follow the directions. [2 points]

> In medieval times rivers were the veins of the body politic as well as economic. Boundaries between states or shires, they were crossed by fords which became the sites of towns, or by bridges which were often points of battle. Upon rivers the people of that time depended for food, _____①_____ and transport. In our day fish are caught in the sea and brought to us by rail and lorry; only the angler still thinks fresh-water fish important, and pollution of rivers drives him into smaller and smaller reaches in which to practice his sport. But in earlier times, when sea fish were eaten only by those who lived on the sea coast, when meat was obtainable only for part of the year, and when fasts were frequent and universally practiced, river fish played an important part in the national life. Every abbey and great man's house had its fish pond, and across the rivers great and small stretched the fish weirs, usually made of stakes and nets or basketwork. Between the owners of the fisheries and the bargemaster who needed an unimpeded passage continuous war was fought, till the importance of freshwater fish lessened as the practice of fasting ceased to be universal, as meat became available all the year round, and as the transport of _____②_____ inland became practicable. Rivers were also the most important source of power. Every stream had its mills, not only for grinding corn, but for all the other industrial processes of the time, such as fulling cloth or driving the hammers of ironworks. Placed down the bank wherever a head of water could be got, these mills were to be found on the tiny stream that ran through a village, or on the bigger river that was also used for navigation.

Fill in the blank ① with the ONE most appropriate word from the passage. Then fill in the blank ② with the TWO most appropriate consecutive words from the passage.

NOTE

Step 1	**S**urvey
Key Words	
Signal Words	
Step 2	**R**eading
Purpose	
Pattern of Organization	
Tone	
Main Idea	
Step 3	**S**ummary
지문 요약하기 (Paraphrasing)	
Step 4	**R**ecite
	요약문 말로 설명하기

19 Read the passage and follow the directions. [2 points]

A new study shows that broad complex developmental changes occur when honey bee larvae—those destined to be workers—are switched from eating royal jelly to a diet of jelly that includes honey and beebread(a type of processed pollen).

Beebread and honey contain p-coumaric acid, but royal jelly does not. Queens feed exclusively on royal jelly. Worker bees known as nurses feed the larvae according to the needs of the hive. Experiments revealed that ingesting p-coumaric acid pushes the honey bee larvae down a different developmental pathway from those fed only royal jelly. Some genes, about a third of the honey bee genome, are upregulated and another third are downregulated, changing the landscape of proteins available to help fight disease or develop the bees' reproductive parts.

Consuming the phytochemical p-coumaric acid, which is ubiquitous in beebread and honey, alters the expression of a whole suite of genes involved in caste determination. For years, people have wondered what components in royal jelly lead to queen development, but what might be more important is what isn't in royal jelly—plant chemicals that can interfere with development.

While previous molecular studies have provided simple snapshots of the gene transcript variations that are associated with the exposure of insects to natural and synthetic chemicals, the genomics approaches used in this study offer a significantly more _____ perspective on the biochemical and physiological processes occurring in plant-insect interactions.

Fill in the blank with the ONE most appropriate word from the passage.

NOTE

Step 1	**S**urvey
Key Words	
Signal Words	
Step 2	**R**eading
Purpose	
Pattern of Organization	
Tone	
Main Idea	
Step 3	**S**ummary
지문 요약하기 (Paraphrasing)	
Step 4	**R**ecite
	요약문 말로 설명하기

20 Read the passage and follow the directions. [2 points]

> There are many sources of false belief besides self-importance. One of these is love of the marvelous. I knew at one time a scientifically-minded conjuror, who used to perform his tricks before a small audience, and then get them, each separately, to write down what they had seen happen. Almost always they wrote down something much more marvelous than the reality, and usually something which no conjuror could have achieved; yet they all thought they were reporting truly what they had seen with their own eyes. This sort of falsification is still more true of rumors. A tells B that last night he saw Mr.-, the eminent prohibitionist, slightly the worse for liquor; B tells C that A saw the good man reeling drunk, C tells D that he was picked up unconscious in the ditch, D tells E that he is well known to pass out every evening. Here, it is true, another motive comes in, namely malice. We like to think ill of our neighbors, and are prepared to believe the worst on very little evidence. But even where there is no such motive, what is _____ is readily believed unless it goes against some strong prejudice. All history until the eighteenth century is full of prodigies and wonders which modern historians ignore, not because they are less well attested than facts which the historians accept, but because modern taste among the learned prefers what science regards as probable.

Fill in the blank with the ONE most appropriate word from the passage.

NOTE

Step 1	Surxvey
Key Words	
Signal Words	
Step 2	**Reading**
Purpose	
Pattern of Organization	
Tone	
Main Idea	
Step 3	**Summary**
지문 요약하기 (Paraphrasing)	
Step 4	**Recite**
	요약문 말로 설명하기

21 Read the passage and follow the directions. [2 points]

> For women, as for girls, intimacy is the fabric of relationships, and talk is the thread from which it is woven. Little girls create and maintain friendships by exchanging secrets; similarly, women regard conversation as the cornerstone of friendship. So a woman expects her husband to be a new and improved version of a best friend. What is important is not the individual subjects that are discussed but the sense of closeness, of a life shared, that emerges when people tell their thoughts, feelings, and impressions. Bonds between boys can be as intense as girls', but they are based less on talking, more on doing things together. Since they don't assume talk is the cement that binds a relationship, men don't know what kind of talk women want, and they don't miss it when it isn't there. Boys' groups are larger, more inclusive, and more hierarchical, so boys must struggle to avoid the subordinate position in the group. This may play a role in women's complaints that men don't listen to them. Some men really don't like to listen, because being the listener makes them feel _____, like a child listening to adults or an employee to a boss.

Fill in the blank with the ONE most appropriate word from the passage.

_____

_____

NOTE

Step 1	Survey
Key Words	
Signal Words	
Step 2	**Reading**
Purpose	
Pattern of Organization	
Tone	
Main Idea	
Step 3	**Summary**
지문 요약하기 (Paraphrasing)	
Step 4	**Recite**

요약문 말로 설명하기

22 Read the passage and follow the directions. [2 points]

> There is lots of zip in DNA-based biology today. With each passing year it incorporates an ever increasing fraction of the life sciences, ranging from single-cell organisms, like bacteria and yeast, to the complexities of the human brain. All this wonderful frenzy was unimaginable when I first entered the world of genetics. In 1948, biology was an all too descriptive discipline near the bottom of science's totem pole, with physics at its top. By then Einstein's turn-of-the century ideas about the interconversion of matter and energy had been transformed into the powers of atom. If not held in check, the nuclear weapons they made possible might well destroy the very fabric of civilized human life. So physicists of the late 1940s were simultaneously revered for making atoms relevant to society and feared for what their toys could do if they were to fall into the hands of evil. Such ambivalent feelings are now widely held toward _____. The double-helical structure of DNA, initially admired for its intellectual simplicity, today represents to many a double-edged sword that can be used for evil as well as good.

Fill in the blank with the ONE most appropriate word from the passage.

_____

_____

NOTE

Step 1	Survey
Key Words	
Signal Words	
Step 2	**Reading**
Purpose	
Pattern of Organization	
Tone	
Main Idea	
Step 3	**Summary**
지문 요약하기 (Paraphrasing)	
Step 4	**Recite**
	요약문 말로 설명하기

23 Read the passage and follow the directions. [2 points]

> For years, critics have argued about the ancient Greek play *Oedipus Rex*. Some have claimed that Oedipus knows nothing of his guilt until the end of the play, when it is revealed that he murdered his own father. Others have insisted that Oedipus is aware all along of his guilt. According to this point of view, Oedipus, the brilliant solver of riddles, could not possibly have ignored the mounting evidence that he was the king's murderer. Just how or why this debate has raged for so many years remains a mystery. The correct interpretations are so obvious. Oedipus knows from the beginning that he is guilty. He just pretends to be ignorant of the truth. For example, when a servant tells the story of the king's murder, he uses the word "bandits." But when Oedipus repeats this story, he uses the singular form "bandit." Sophocles provides clues like this throughout the play. Thus, it's hard to understand why anyone would think that Oedipus does not know the _____.

Fill in the blank with the ONE most appropriate word from the passage.

NOTE

Step 1	**S**urvey
Key Words	
Signal Words	
Step 2	**R**eading
Purpose	
Pattern of Organization	
Tone	
Main Idea	
Step 3	**S**ummary
지문 요약하기 (Paraphrasing)	
Step 4	**R**ecite
	요약문 말로 설명하기

24 Read the passage and follow the directions. [2 points]

> Pain has plagued us throughout the history of our species. We spend our lives trying to avoid it, and, from one point of view, what we call "happiness" may be just the absence of pain. Yet it is difficult to describe pain, which may be sharp, dull, shooting, throbbing, imaginary, or referred. We have many pains that surge from within as cramps and aches. And we also talk about emotional distress as pain. Pains are often combined, the emotional with the physical, and the physical with the physical. When you burn yourself, the skin swells and blisters, and when the blister breaks, the skin hurts in yet another way. A wound may become infected. Then histamine and serotonin are released, which dilate the blood vessels and trigger a pain response. Not all internal injuries can be felt (it's possible to do brain surgery under a local anesthetic), but illnesses that constrict blood flow often are: Angina pectoris, for example, which occurs when the coronary arteries shrink too tight for blood to comfortably pass. Even intense pain often eludes accurate description, as Virginia Woolf reminds us in her essay "On Being Ill": "English, which can express the thoughts of Hamlet and the tragedy of Lear, has few words for the shiver and the headache ... let a sufferer try to _____ a pain in his head to a doctor and language at once runs dry."

Fill in the blank with the ONE most appropriate word from the passage.

_____

_____

NOTE

Step 1	**S**urvey
Key Words	
Signal Words	
Step 2	**R**eading
Purpose	
Pattern of Organization	
Tone	
Main Idea	
Step 3	**S**ummary
지문 요약하기 (Paraphrasing)	
Step 4	**R**ecite
	요약문 말로 설명하기

25 **Read the passage and follow the directions.** [2 points]

> People are always talking about the _____ of youth. If there is one—which I take leave to doubt—then, it is older people who create it, not the young themselves. Let us get down to fundamentals and agree that the young are after all human beings—people just like their elders. There is only one difference between an old man and a young one: the young man has a glorious future before him and the old one has a splendid future behind him: and maybe that is where the rub is. When I was a teenager, I felt that I was just young and uncertain—that I was a new boy in a huge school, and I would have been very pleased to be regarded as something so interesting as a problem. For one thing, being a problem gives you a certain identity, and that is one of the things the young are busily engaged in seeking. I find young people exciting. They have an air of freedom, and they have not a dreary commitment to mean ambitions or love of comfort. They are not anxious social climbers, and they have no devotion to material things. All this seems to me to link them with life, and the origins of things. It's as if they were in some sense cosmic beings in violent and lovely contrast with us suburban creatures. All that is in my mind when I meet a young person. He may be conceited, illmannered, presumptuous or fatuous, but I do not turn for protection to dreary clichés about respect for elders—as if mere age were a reason for respect. I accept that we are equals, and I will argue with him, as an equal, if I think he is wrong.

Fill in the blank with the ONE most appropriate word from the passage.

NOTE

Step 1	**S**urvey
Key Words	
Signal Words	
Step 2	**R**eading
Purpose	
Pattern of Organization	
Tone	
Main Idea	
Step 3	**S**ummary
지문 요약하기 (Paraphrasing)	
Step 4	**R**ecite
	요약문 말로 설명하기

2S2R

유희태 일반영어
② 유형

PART 02

서술형

A형 서술형

01 Read the passage and follow the directions. [4 points]

> Like most of my generation, I was brought up on the saying: "Satan finds some mischief for idle hands to do." Being a highly virtuous child, I believed all that I was told, and acquired a conscience which has kept me working hard down to the present moment. But although my conscience has controlled my actions, my opinions have undergone a revolution. I think that there is far too much work done in the world and that what needs to be preached in modern industrial countries is quite different from what always has been preached. Everyone knows the story of the traveler in Naples who saw twelve beggars lying in the sun (it was before the days of Mussolini), and offered a lira to the idlest of them. Eleven of them jumped up to claim it, so he gave it to the twelfth. <u>This traveler was on the right lines</u>. But in countries which do not enjoy Mediterranean sunshine idleness is more difficult, and a great public propaganda will be required to inaugurate it. I hope that the leaders of the YMCA will start a campaign to induce good young men to do nothing. If so, I shall not have lived in vain.

Complete the idea that the writer is conveying by filling in the blank with the ONE most appropriate word from the passage. Second, explain what the underlined part means.

> Immense harm is caused by the belief that much work is _____.

NOTE

Step 1	**S**urvey
Key Words	
Signal Words	
Step 2	**R**eading
Purpose	
Pattern of Organization	
Tone	
Main Idea	
Step 3	**S**ummary
지문 요약하기 (Paraphrasing)	
Step 4	**R**ecite
	요약문 말로 설명하기

02 Read the passage and follow the directions. [4 points]

Sunlight is not the only forceful breeze that emanates from the Sun. There is another, known as the solar wind. The solar wind is a flood of plasma, protons and electrons, that streams out constantly from the Sun in all directions at a velocity of about 500 hm/s. We never encounter it here on Earth, because we are protected from it by the Earth's magnetosphere.

If the Earth's magnetosphere blocks the solar wind, it must be creating drag, and therefore feel a force as a result. Why not create an artificial magnetosphere on a spacecraft and use the same effect for propulsion? This was an idea that Boeing engineer Dana Andrews and I hit on in 1988. The idea was timely. In 1987, high-temperature superconductors had been discovered. These are essential to making a magnetic propulsion device practical, as low-temperature superconductors require too much heavy cooling equipment and ordinary conductors require too much power. The amount of force per square kilometer of solar wind is much less than that created by sunlight, but the area blocked off by a magnetic field could be made much larger than any practical solid solar sail. Working in collaboration, Dana and I derived equations and ran computer simulations of the solar wind impacting a spacecraft generating a large magnetic field.

Our results: If practical high-temperature superconducting cable can be made that can conduct electrical current with the same density as the state-of-the-art low-temperature superconductors such as niobium titanium, then magnetic sails or "magsails" can be made that will have thrust-to-weight ratios a hundred times better than that of a 10-micron-thick solar sail. Furthermore, unlike an ultra-thin solar sail, the _____ would not be difficult to deploy. Instead of being made of thin plastic film, they would be made of rugged cable, which due to magnetic forces would automatically "inflate" itself into a stiff hoop shape as soon as electrical current was put in it.

Fill in the blank with the TWO most appropriate consecutive words from the passage. Second, explain why "The idea" was favorable.

_____

_____

NOTE

Step 1	**S**urvey
Key Words	
Signal Words	
Step 2	**R**eading
Purpose	
Pattern of Organization	
Tone	
Main Idea	
Step 3	**S**ummary
지문 요약하기 (Paraphrasing)	
Step 4	**R**ecite
	요약문 말로 설명하기

03 Read the passage and follow the directions. [4 points]

> Fathers' rights as a civil liberties issue seems like a laughable bemoaning of one's patriarchal privilege. It appears anti-feminist: It's mostly men who run the world, no matter what Beyonce sings. But despite male dominance of government and business, disparities in pay and household responsibility and even continued risk of sexual assault, real examples of male inequality should not be dismissed.
>
> Unmarried men have little security in child rearing decisions and custody outcomes. Legally, the extent of decisions made by married men about reproduction and children stops at the sexual act. Beyond that, the mother has the most leverage to make decisions about visitation and possible adoption. Why? Because law and social practice assume that _____ in intimate relationships have no interest in commitment, stability or responsibility.
>
> Of course, individuals and institutions have stories and numbers to "prove" that fathers should be treated differently than mothers because they're irresponsible. Old laws are illustrative of this assumption: Unmarried fathers would lose custody of their children upon the death of their mother, because the law deemed them inherently unfit, incapable and unstable. In a majority of states, adoptions can proceed even without the knowledge of the birth father, unless they can miraculously register as a putative father in advance of the birth.
>
> But is it fair to characterize all unmarried men as deadbeats, just because they are not married? If men want fair treatment, this doesn't inherently mean they oppose women's equality or advancement. There are always going to be bad examples of fed up, angry, bitter men that spout invectives at feminists, their ex-wives and all women in general. But <u>all papas are not rolling stones</u>. There are just regular, earnest, nice guys that want simple due process rights as men and partners.

2S2R 유형

Fill in the blank with the TWO most appropriate consecutive words from the passage. Second, explain what the underlined "all papas are not rolling stones" means.

___

___

NOTE

Step 1	**S**urvey
Key Words	
Signal Words	
Step 2	**R**eading
Purpose	
Pattern of Organization	
Tone	
Main Idea	
Step 3	**S**ummary
지문 요약하기 (Paraphrasing)	
Step 4	**R**ecite
	요약문 말로 설명하기

A형 서술형 65

04 Read the passage and follow the directions. [4 points]

> "To have" is a deceptively simple expression. Every human being has something: a body, clothes, shelter—on up to the modern man or woman who has a car, a television set, a washing machine, etc. Living without having something is virtually impossible. Why then should having be a problem? Yet the linguistic history of "having" indicates that the word is indeed a problem. To those who believe that to have is a most natural category of human existence, it may come as a surprise to learn that many languages have no word for "to have." In Hebrew, for instance, "I have" must be expressed by the indirect form *jesh li* ("there is to me"). In fact, languages that express possession in this way rather than by "I have," predominate. It is interesting to note that in the development of many languages, the construction "there is to me" is followed later on by the construction "I have," but as Emile Benveniste has pointed out, the evolution does not occur in the reverse direction. This fact suggests that the word for "to have" develops in connection with the development of private property, while it is absent in societies with predominantly functional property, that is, possession for use.

Identify to what the underlined "the reverse direction" refers. Second, explain what the underlined ""To have" is a deceptively simple expression" means.

NOTE

Step 1	**S**urvey
Key Words	
Signal Words	
Step 2	**R**eading
Purpose	
Pattern of Organization	
Tone	
Main Idea	
Step 3	**S**ummary
지문 요약하기 (Paraphrasing)	
Step 4	**R**ecite
	요약문 말로 설명하기

05 Read the passage and follow the directions. [4 points]

    Modern European and American history is centered around the effort to gain freedom from the political, economic, and spiritual shackles that have bound men. The battles for freedom were fought by the _____, those who wanted new liberties, against those who had privileges to defend. While a class was fighting for its own liberation from domination, it believed itself to be fighting for human freedom as such and thus was able to appeal to an ideal, to the longing for freedom rooted in all who are oppressed. Despite many reversals, freedom has won battles. Many died in those battles in the conviction that to die in the struggle against oppression was better than to live without freedom. Such a death was the utmost assertion of their individuality. History seemed to be proving that it was possible for man to govern himself, to make decisions for himself, and to think and feel as he saw fit. The full expression of man's potentialities seemed to be the goal towards which social development was rapidly approaching. The principles of economic liberalism, political democracy, religious autonomy, and individualism in personal life, gave expression to the longing for freedom, and at the same time seemed to bring mankind nearer to its realization. <u>One tie after another</u> was severed. Man had overthrown the domination of nature and made himself her master; he had overthrown the domination of the Church and the domination of the absolutist state. The abolition of external domination seemed to be not only a necessary but also a sufficient condition to attain the cherished goal: freedom of the individual.

Fill in the blank with the ONE most appropriate word from the passage. Second, identify to what the underlined phrase "One tie after another" refers.

NOTE

Step 1	**S**urvey
Key Words	
Signal Words	
Step 2	**R**eading
Purpose	
Pattern of Organization	
Tone	
Main Idea	
Step 3	**S**ummary
지문 요약하기 (Paraphrasing)	
Step 4	**R**ecite
	요약문 말로 설명하기

06 Read the passage and follow the directions. [4 points]

> The newspaper must provide for the reader the facts, unslanted, objectively selected facts. But in these days of complex news it must provide more; it must supply interpretation, the meaning of the facts. This is the most important assignment confronting American journalism—to make clear to the reader the problems of the day, to make international news as understandable as community news, to recognize that there is no longer any such thing as "local" news, because any event in the international area has a local reaction in manpower draft, in economic strain, in terms, indeed, of our very way of life. There is in journalism a widespread view that when you embark on interpretation, you are entering choppy and dangerous waters, the swirling tides of opinion. This is nonsense.
>
> The opponents of interpretation insist that the writer and the editor shall confine themselves to the "facts." This insistence raises two questions. As to the first query, consider how a so-called "factual" story comes about. The reporter collects, say, fifty facts; out of these fifty, his space allotment being necessarily restricted, he selects the ten, which he considers most important. This is Judgment Number One. Then he or his editor decides which of these ten facts shall constitute the lead of the piece. This is important decision because many readers do not proceed beyond the first paragraph. This is Judgment Number Two. Then the night editor determines whether the article shall be presented on page one, where it has a large impact, or on page twenty-four, where it has little. Judgment Number Three.

Thus, in the presentation of a so-called "factual" or "objective" story, at least three judgments are involved. And they are judgments not at all unlike those involved in _____, in which reporter and editor, calling upon their general background, and their "news neutralism", arrive at a conclusion as to the significance of the news. The two areas of judgment, presentation of the news and its interpretation, are both objective rather than subjective processes—as objective, that is, as any human being can be. If an editor is intent on slanting the news, he can do it in other ways and more effectively than by interpretation. He can do it by the selection of those facts that prop up his particular plea. Or he can do it by the play he gives a story—promoting it to page one or demoting it to page thirty.

Describe what "Judgment Number One" and what "Judgment Number Three" are. Also, in what way are presentation and interpretation of news similar? While making your answer, do not copy more than FOUR consecutive words from the passage. Third, fill in the blank with the ONE most appropriate word from the passage.

_____
_____
_____
_____

NOTE

Step 1	**S**urvey
Key Words	
Signal Words	
Step 2	**R**eading
Purpose	
Pattern of Organization	
Tone	
Main Idea	
Step 3	**S**ummary
지문 요약하기 (Paraphrasing)	
Step 4	**R**ecite
	요약문 말로 설명하기

MEMO

07 Read the passage and follow the directions. [4 points]

Personal independence is such an iconic American value today that few of us question it. In previous generations, retirees lived with family, but now that a large swath of older people can afford to live on their own, that's what they choose. The convenience of digital devices means that we can now work, shop and pay our bills online, without dealing directly with other people. 10% of Americans work alone in remote offices and over 13% live alone, the highest rate of solo living in American history.

Many researches, however, suggest that, even if you enjoy being by yourself, it just might kill you—or at least shorten your life. Living alone, or simply spending a lot of your time on your own, can compromise your physical and psychological resilience—whether or not you like your solitude. If you fit into one of following categories—living alone, spending much of your time alone or often feeling solitary—your risk of dying within the next seven years is about 30% higher than it is for people who are otherwise like you. In-person interaction has physiological effects.

① A landmark longitudinal study published in the American Journal of Epidemiology in 1979 followed nearly every resident of a northern California town for nine years; its results showed that people who not only had intimate partners but met regularly with others to play bridge or volunteer at church were twice as likely to outlive those who led _____②_____ lives. Still, critics wondered whether social contact was the key. Perhaps the social butterflies were healthier to begin with, or the more isolated people had hidden problems, such as depression or disability, that cut their lives short. A team led by Dr. Julianne Holt controlled for these confounding factors. What's more, they discovered that the effect isn't always a matter of preference or state of mind. We used to think that subjective experience was all that mattered. You could be single or married, spend your days alone or in a throng of people; if you often felt lonely, the thinking went, your blood pressure would spike and your immune function would suffer.

The new research found, however, that objective measures of the amount of human contact you get are as critical to your survival as your opinion of your social life. "I've spent almost my whole career studying social support, and I absolutely know the strong effects that our perceptions have on our physiology," Dr. Holt said. "But there are other determinants of health that are independent of our perceptions.

Describe what the "A landmark longitudinal study" discovered regarding lifespan. Also, how is the study led by Dr. Holt is different from the landmark study? When you answer these questions, do not copy more than FIVE consecutive words from the passage. Third, fill in the blank with the ONE most appropriate word from the passage.

NOTE

Step 1	Survey
Key Words	
Signal Words	
Step 2	**Reading**
Purpose	
Pattern of Organization	
Tone	
Main Idea	
Step 3	**Summary**
지문 요약하기 (Paraphrasing)	
Step 4	**Recite**
	요약문 말로 설명하기

MEMO

08 Read the passage and follow the directions. [4 points]

Whether they trust it or not, consumers aren't exactly avoiding G.M. foods, at least in some places. It's hard to find a soybean or a kernel of corn in North America that's not genetically modified. That G.M. foods are so prevalent in the region may not be realized because American food providers are not required to disclose G.M.O. content. There seems to be little clamor for such information, either; in a 2012 referendum in health-conscious California, voters narrowly declined to require labeling. Labeling rules are stricter in Europe, and far less G.M. food is produced or consumed there. A European Commission decision in April allowing member states to restrict the use of G.M.O.s approved at the regional level suggests that the public isn't warming to them.

G.M. crops are becoming more prevalent in the developing world, however. Their use is permitted across Latin America, Asia and Africa. Brazil is the second-largest producer, after the United States, followed by Argentina. Extensive cultivation of G.M.O.s also occurs in China, Paraguay and South Africa. In 2012, for the first time, the area planted with G.M. crops in developing countries was higher than in developed countries. Their grip hasn't loosened since then. Farmers in the developing world planted about 95 million hectares (235 million acres) of G.M. crops in 2014, five times more than in 2003. That compares with a doubling in industrial countries, to about 86 million hectares. One reason for the appeal in emerging economies is clear. Increases in yields and profits with G.M. crops were substantially greater there than in mature economies. The developing world is also where a lot of hunger exists, and much hope is being pinned on the success of G.M. crops to alleviate it.

But as with other aspects of G.M.O.s, doubts have been raised about their utility in reducing hunger and increasing the global food supply. Some researchers contend that indoor farming can do both in a more benign way. Having total control over light, water and other factors allows food to grow much faster than outdoors, they say. The United Nations World Food Program makes the case that limited supply isn't the primary reason for food shortages. Lack of investment in infrastructure that gets food from where it's grown to where it's eaten is a bigger culprit as are wastage and war.

2S2R 유형

Explain TWO reasons why G.M. crops appeal to less developed countries. Also, according to the United Nation World Food Program, what are the primary reasons for food shortages among developing countries?

_____

_____

NOTE

Step 1	Survey
Key Words	
Signal Words	
Step 2	**Reading**
Purpose	
Pattern of Organization	
Tone	
Main Idea	
Step 3	**Summary**
지문 요약하기 (Paraphrasing)	
Step 4	**Recite**
	요약문 말로 설명하기

A형 서술형 79

09 Read the passage and follow the directions. [4 points]

> Benjamin Blencowe and his team have recently uncovered how a small change in a protein called PTBP1 can spur the creation of neurons—cells that make the brain—that could have fuelled the evolution of mammalian brains to become the largest and most complex among vertebrates.
>
> Brain size and complexity vary enormously across vertebrates, but it is not clear how these differences came about. Humans and frogs, for example, have been evolving separately for 350 million years and have very different brain abilities. Yet scientists have shown that they use a remarkably similar repertoire of genes to build organs in the body.
>
> So how is it that a similar number of genes, that are also switched on or off in similar ways in diverse vertebrate species, generate a vast range of organ size and complexity?
>
> The key lays in the process that Blencowe's group studies, known as alternative splicing (AS), whereby gene products are assembled into proteins, which are the building blocks of life. During AS, gene fragments —called exons—are shuffled to make different protein shapes. It's like LEGO, where some fragments can be missing from the final protein shape.
>
> AS enables cells to make more than one protein from a single gene, so that the total number of different proteins in a cell greatly surpasses the number of available genes. A cell's ability to regulate protein diversity at any given time reflects its ability to take on different roles in the body. AS prevalence increases with vertebrate complexity. So although the genes that make bodies of vertebrates might be similar, the _____ they give rise to are far more diverse in animals such as mammals, than in birds and frogs. And nowhere is AS more widespread than in the brain.

Describe what alternative splicing is and explain why it could be the key to how human beings evolved to become the smartest animal on the planet. Second, fill in the blank with the ONE most appropriate word from the passage.

_____

_____

NOTE

Step 1	**S**urvey
Key Words	
Signal Words	
Step 2	**R**eading
Purpose	
Pattern of Organization	
Tone	
Main Idea	
Step 3	**S**ummary
지문 요약하기 (Paraphrasing)	
Step 4	**R**ecite
	요약문 말로 설명하기

10 Read the passage and follow the directions. [4 points]

> Two traits that set humans apart from other primates—big brains and the ability to walk upright—could be at odds when it comes to childbirth. Big brains and the big heads that encase them are hard to push through the human birth canal, but a wider pelvis might compromise bipedal walking. Scientists have long posited that nature's solution to this problem, which is known as the "obstetric dilemma," was to shorten the duration of gestation so that babies are born before their heads get too big. As a result, human babies are relatively helpless and seemingly underdeveloped in terms of motor and cognitive ability compared to other primates.
>
> All these fascinating phenomena in human evolution—bipedalism, difficult childbirth, wide female hips, big brains, relatively helpless babies—have traditionally been tied together with the obstetric dilemma. It's been taught in anthropology courses for decades, but when I looked for hard evidence that it's actually true, I struck out.
>
> The problem with the theory is that there is no evidence that hips wide enough to deliver a more developed baby would be a detriment to walking. That throws doubt on the assumption that the size of the birth canal is limited by bipedalism. Wide hips don't mean you can't walk efficiently. Controlling for mother's body size, human gestation is a bit longer than expected compared to other primates, not shorter. And babies are a bit larger than expected, not smaller. Although babies behave like it, they're not born early.

For mammals in general, including humans, gestation length and offspring size are predicted by mother's body size. Because body size is a good proxy for an animal's metabolic rate and function, metabolism might offer a better explanation for the timing of human birth than the pelvis. Women give birth just as they are about to cross into a metabolic danger zone. During pregnancy, women approach that energetic ceiling and give birth right before they reach it. That suggests there is an energetic limit to human gestation length and fetal growth. Those metabolic constraints help explain why human babies are so helpless compared to our primate kin, like chimpanzees. A chimp baby begins crawling at one month, whereas human babies don't crawl until around seven months. But for a human to give birth to a newborn at the same developmental level as chimp, it would take a 16-month gestation. That would place mothers well past their _____.
In fact, even one extra month of gestation would cross into the metabolic danger zone.

*bipedalism: walking on two legs

The writer of the passage refutes long-held theory on human gestation. First, describe what the long-held theory is. Second, according to the author, why are human babies relatively helpless and underdeveloped compared to other primates? When you answer, do NOT copy more than FIVE consecutive words from the passage. Third, fill in the blank with the TWO most appropriate consecutive words from the passage.

_____
_____
_____
_____

NOTE

Step 1	Survey
Key Words	
Signal Words	
Step 2	**Reading**
Purpose	
Pattern of Organization	
Tone	
Main Idea	
Step 3	**Summary**
지문 요약하기 (Paraphrasing)	
Step 4	**Recite**
	요약문 말로 설명하기

MEMO

11 Read the passage and follow the directions. [4 points]

> With the rise of the great metropolis in the industrial era, city planning in the West passed out of the hands of the architect and into the hands of the technocrat. Unlike the architect who thought of the city as a work of art to be built up with an eye toward beauty, the technocrat has always taken a purely functional approach to city planning: the city exists for the sole purpose of serving the needs of its inhabitants. Its outward appearance has no intrinsic value.
>
> Over the span of a few centuries, this new breed of urban planner has succeeded in forever changing the face of the Western city. A brief visit to any large metropolis is enough to confirm this grim fact. Even a casual observer could not fail to notice that the typical urban landscape is arranged along the lines of the tedious chessboard pattern, with its fourcornered intersections and long, straight and dull streets. Strict building codes have resulted in an overabundance of unsightly neighborhoods in which there is only slight variation among structures. Rows of squat concrete apartment houses and files of gigantic steel and glass skyscrapers have almost completely replaced older, more personal buildings. Moreover, the lovely natural surroundings of many cities are no longer a part of the urban landscape. For the most part, the hills and rivers which were once so much a part of so many metropolitan settings have now been blotted out by primarily _____①_____ construction.
>
> The lone bright spot amidst all of this urban blight has been the local park system, which is to be found in most Western cities. Large, centrally-located parks—for example, New York's Central Park or London's Hyde Park—and smaller, outlying parks bring a measure of beauty to Western cities by breaking up the man-made monotony. With their green pastures, dense woods, and pleasant ponds, streams and waterfalls, local park systems also offer a vast array of opportunities for city dwellers to rest or recreate, free of the intense burdens of urban life. If they have understood nothing else about the quality of life in urban areas, technocrats have at least had ② the good sense to recognize that people need a quiet refuge from the chaotic bustle of the city.

The writer of the passage, in the first paragraph, contrasts architects to technocrats. Explain this difference in ONE sentence. Second, what does the underlined part suggest about technocrats? Write your answer in 10 words or so. When you answer the questions, do NOT copy more than FIVE consecutive words from the passage. Third, fill in the blank with the ONE most appropriate word from the passage.

_____

_____

NOTE

Step 1	**S**urvey
Key Words	
Signal Words	
Step 2	**R**eading
Purpose	
Pattern of Organization	
Tone	
Main Idea	
Step 3	**S**ummary
지문 요약하기 (Paraphrasing)	
Step 4	**R**ecite
	요약문 말로 설명하기

12 Read the passage and follow the directions. [4 points]

> The line between a prejudiced belief and a merely controversial one is elusive, and the harder you look the more elusive it becomes. "God hates homosexuals" is a statement of fact, not of bias, to those who believe it; "American criminals are disproportionately black" is a statement of bias, not of fact, to those who disbelieve it. Who is right? You may decide, and so may others, and there is no need to agree. That is the great innovation of _____. We cannot know in advance or for sure which belief is prejudice and which is truth, but to advance knowledge we don't need to know. The genius of intellectual pluralism lies not in doing away with prejudices and dogmas but in channeling them—making them socially productive by pitting prejudice against prejudice and dogma against dogma, exposing all to withering public criticism. What survives at the end of the day is our base of knowledge.

Fill in the blank with the TWO most appropriate consecutive words from the passage. Second, outline the writer's reason for defending prejudice.

_____
_____
_____
_____

NOTE

Step 1	**S**urvey
Key Words	
Signal Words	
Step 2	**R**eading
Purpose	
Pattern of Organization	
Tone	
Main Idea	
Step 3	**S**ummary
지문 요약하기 (Paraphrasing)	
Step 4	**R**ecite
	요약문 말로 설명하기

13 Read the passage and follow the directions. [4 points]

> The lives of insects, at the broadest level, are organized to produce the greatest number of offspring that are mature and successful. This number defines an insect's fitness. There are many ways to maximize fitness, but they all involve economizing time and energy, the common currencies of life. Time and energy budgets are shaped, evolutionarily, according to the principles of stringency and allocation. This means that the budgets are geared to fit the worst conditions an insect might encounter and that time and energy are allocated among survival and reproductive activities so as to maximize fitness. Each sex of an insect species typically allocates a certain portion of its time carrying out several necessary activities, such as feeding, nest making, mating, grooming, and quiescence. Quiescence serves to avoid natural enemies, inimical weather, or stressful times of day, while important internal activities continue, such as food digestion. The energy obtained by feeding is likewise budgeted among several activities that compete for energy use, such as metabolic activity, formation of sperm or eggs, locomotion, and behaviors for obtaining specific nutrients, finding mates, and defense. The best budgets are those that lead to the largest _____ and become propagated through natural selection. Thus we assume that the way insects organize and distribute their behaviors is roughly optimized for a particular insect niche.

Write the THREE most appropriate consecutive words from the passage that best fit in the blank. Second, explain the importance of quiescence in an insect's energy budget as described in the passage.

_____
_____
_____
_____

NOTE

Step 1	**S**urvey
Key Words	
Signal Words	
Step 2	**R**eading
Purpose	
Pattern of Organization	
Tone	
Main Idea	
Step 3	**S**ummary
지문 요약하기 (Paraphrasing)	
Step 4	**R**ecite
	요약문 말로 설명하기

14 Read the passage and follow the directions. [4 points]

> It has long been assumed that cultural bias in assigning and reinforcing gender roles has led to an unfair characterization of women as more apt to complain and less able to bear pain. Boys are raised in many places not to show pain, but instead, as an exhibition of strength, to remain passive before it. Recent research suggests, however, that men and women actually experience pain differently. It has long been known, for instance, that men and women each prefer different classes of painkillers and that these painkillers morphine and nalbuphine treat two different parts of the brain. It has also been shown that babies show different responses to pain within six hours of birth, and that rats and mice have clear gender differences in how they respond to the same stimuli.
>
> The most recent research shows that not only are migraines three times more common in women than men, but that it might be associated with a lowered pain threshold but only in women. A Canadian geneticist who conducted part of this research also isolated a gene that, in women, affects their sensitivity to and ability to tolerate pain. It had no effect on men. He now believes that male and female brains actually process painful stimuli using wholly different sets of neurons and neurotransmitters. In conjunction with the other evidence and well-known surveys showing that women report feeling more pain, more frequently in more parts of their body and for longer periods than men, it might not simply be cultural bias but actual genetics that dictates that "boys don't cry."

In the above passage, explain the key evidence used to argue that both sexes experience pain differently. Then, explain the meaning of the underlined expression.

_____
_____
_____
_____

NOTE

Step 1	**S**urvey
Key Words	
Signal Words	
Step 2	**R**eading
Purpose	
Pattern of Organization	
Tone	
Main Idea	
Step 3	**S**ummary
지문 요약하기 (Paraphrasing)	
Step 4	**R**ecite
	요약문 말로 설명하기

15 Read the passage and follow the directions. [4 points]

> Mohammad Yunus of Bangladesh, founder of the Grameen Bank and the main inventor of microcredit schemes, didn't start off with the goal of giving poor people credit. Initially he started off with the conviction that the Green Revolution, and irrigation, was the answer to poverty in Bangladesh. His doctoral dissertation at Vanderbilt University was titled "Optimal Allocation of Multi-Purpose Reservoir Water: A Dynamic Programming Model." His first attempt to help the poor was to sponsor tube wells for irrigation during the dry season so farmers could grow two crops a year. Yunus gave the farmers a loan out of his own money to finance the scheme. The farmers reaped a good harvest. <u>Ironically</u> for the founder of the idea that the poor can be a good credit risk, the farmers didn't fully repay Yunus, and he lost money.
>
> Yunus persisted, visiting as many rural villages as possible to try to understand how to help. He then encountered a woman named Sufiya Begum making a bamboo stool. Begum made a pitiful two cents on every stool, mainly because a moneylender charged her a very high interest rate to advance her the bamboo. Yunus realized that very small loans to very poor people could make a big difference in their lives. He experimented, and found that microcredit borrowers would repay the loan in order to get access to future loans. His first loan at the Grameen Bank was to Sufiya, who started a successful peddling business with the money. There was a huge demand for such loans, and the Grameen Bank became the legend that it is today with imitators from all over the world.

Explain the meaning of the underlined "Ironically". Second, describe the way that Yunus incentivized loan payback.

_____
_____
_____
_____
_____

NOTE

Step 1	Survey
Key Words	
Signal Words	
Step 2	**Reading**
Purpose	
Pattern of Organization	
Tone	
Main Idea	
Step 3	**Summary**
지문 요약하기 (Paraphrasing)	
Step 4	**Recite**
	요약문 말로 설명하기

16 Read the passage and follow the directions. [4 points]

> One kind of ____①____ deserves special mention. This is the mistake that arises from the misuse of relative terms, which have different meanings in different contexts. For example, the word "tall" is a relative word; a tall man and a tall building are in quite different categories. A tall man is one who is taller than most men; a tall building is one that is taller than most buildings. Certain forms of argument that are valid for nonrelative terms break down when relative terms are substituted for them. The argument "an elephant is an animal; therefore a gray elephant is a gray animal" is perfectly valid. The word "gray" is a nonrelative term. But the argument "an elephant is an animal; therefore a small elephant is a small animal" is ridiculous. The point here is that "small" is a relative term: A small elephant is a very large animal. The fallacy is one of equivocation with regard to the relative term "small". Not all equivocation on relative terms is so obvious, however. The word "good" is a relative term and is frequently equivocated on when it is argued, for example, that so-and-so is a good general and would therefore be a good president, or that ② someone is a good scholar and is therefore likely to be a good teacher.

Fill in the blank with the ONE most appropriate word from the passage. Second, explain why the writer uses the example "someone is a good scholar and is therefore likely to be a good teacher' in the final sentence."

NOTE

Step 1	**S**urvey
Key Words	
Signal Words	
Step 2	**R**eading
Purpose	
Pattern of Organization	
Tone	
Main Idea	
Step 3	**S**ummary
지문 요약하기 (Paraphrasing)	
Step 4	**R**ecite
	요약문 말로 설명하기

17 Read the passage and follow the directions. [4 points]

> Faith in progress is deep within our American culture. We have been taught to believe that our lives are better than the lives of those who came before us. The ideology of modern economics suggests that material progress has yielded enhanced satisfaction and well-being. But much of our confidence about our own well-being comes from the assumption that our lives are easier than those of earlier generations. I have already disputed the notion that we work less than medieval European peasants, however poor they may have been. The field research of anthropologists gives another view of ① the conventional wisdom. The lives of so-called primitive peoples are commonly thought to be harsh—their existence dominated by the "incessant quest for food." In fact, primitives do little work. By contemporary standards, we'd have to judge them very lazy. If the Kapauku of Papua work one day, they do no labor on the next. Kung Bushmen put in only two and a half days per week and six hours per day. In the Sandwich Islands of Hawaii, men work only four hours per day. And Australian aborigines have similar schedules. The key to understanding why these ② "Stone-Age peoples" fail to act like us—increasing their work effort to get more things—is that they have limited desires. In the race between wanting and having, they have kept their wanting low. In this way, they ensure their own kind of satisfaction. They are materially poor by contemporary standards, but in at least one dimension—time—we have to count them richer.

Describe what "the conventional wisdom" is. Also, explain how "Stone-Age peoples" ensures their satisfaction.

NOTE

Step 1	**S**urvey
Key Words	
Signal Words	
Step 2	**R**eading
Purpose	
Pattern of Organization	
Tone	
Main Idea	
Step 3	**S**ummary
지문 요약하기 (Paraphrasing)	
Step 4	**R**ecite
	요약문 말로 설명하기

18 Read the passage and follow the directions. [4 points]

> The common belief of some linguists that each language is a(n) _____①_____ vehicle for the thoughts of the nation speaking it is in some ways the exact counterpart of the conviction of the Manchester school of economics that supply and demand will regulate everything for the best. Just as economists were blind to the numerous cases in which the law of supply and demand left actual wants unsatisfied, so also many linguists are deaf to those instances in which the very nature of a language calls forth misunderstandings in everyday conversation, and in which, consequently, a word has to be modified or defined in order to present the idea intended by the speaker: ② "He took his stick—no, not John's, but his own." No language is perfect, and if we admit this truth we must also admit that it is not unreasonable to investigate the relative merits of different languages or of different details in languages.

Fill in the blank with the ONE most appropriate word from the passage. Second, what contributes to the misunderstanding described by the author in the underlined part "He took his stick—no, not John's, but his own."?

NOTE

Step 1	**S**urvey
Key Words	
Signal Words	
Step 2	**R**eading
Purpose	
Pattern of Organization	
Tone	
Main Idea	
Step 3	**S**ummary
지문 요약하기 (Paraphrasing)	
Step 4	**R**ecite
	요약문 말로 설명하기

19 **Read the passage and follow the directions.** [4 points]

　　When I was teaching English at the Colorado Rocky Mountain School, I used to ask my students the kinds of questions that English teachers usually ask about reading assignments—questions designed to bring out the points that I had decided they should know. They, on their part, would try to get me to give them hints and clues as to what I wanted. It was a game of wits. I never gave my students an opportunity to say what they really thought about a book. I gave vocabulary drills and quizzes too. I told my students that every time they came upon a word in their book they did not understand, they were to look it up in the dictionary. I even devised special kinds of vocabulary tests, allowing them to use their books to see how the words were used. But looking back, I realize that ① these tests, along with many of my methods, were foolish. My sister was the first person who made me question my conventional ideas about teaching English. She had a son in the seventh grade in a fairly good public school. His teacher had asked the class to read Cooper's *The Deerslayer*. The choice was bad enough in itself; whether looking at man or nature, Cooper was superficial, inaccurate and sentimental, and his writing is ponderous and ornate. But to make matters worse, this teacher had decided to give the book the microscope and X-ray treatment. He made the students look up and memorize not only the definitions but the derivations of every big word that came along—and there were plenty. Every chapter was followed by close questioning and testing to make sure the students "understood" everything. Being then, as I said, _____②_____, I began to defend the teacher, who was a good friend of mine, against my sister's criticisms. The argument soon grew hot. What was wrong with making sure that children understood everything they read? My sister answered that until this year her boy had always loved reading, and had read a lot on his own; now he had stopped. He was not really to start again for many years.

2S2R 유형

Explain the reason the writer thinks the underlined "these tests" were unwise. Second, fill in the blank with the ONE most appropriate word from the passage.

_____

_____

NOTE

Step 1	**S**urvey
Key Words	
Signal Words	
Step 2	**R**eading
Purpose	
Pattern of Organization	
Tone	
Main Idea	
Step 3	**S**ummary
지문 요약하기 (Paraphrasing)	
Step 4	**R**ecite
	요약문 말로 설명하기

A형 서술형

20 Read the passage and follow the directions. [4 points]

It is very easy to argue that ① knowledge about Shakespeare or Wordsworth is not political whereas knowledge about contemporary China or North Korea is. My own formal and professional designation is that of "humanist", a title which indicates the humanities as my field and therefore the unlikely eventuality that there might be anything political about what I do in that field. Of course, all these labels and terms are quite unnuanced as I use them here, but the general truth of what I am pointing to is widely held. One reason for saying that a humanist who writes about Wordsworth or an editor whose specialty is Keats is not involved in anything political is that what he does seems to have no direct political effect upon reality in the everyday sense. A scholar whose field is Chinese economics works in a highly charged area where there is much government interest, and what he might produce in the way of studies or proposals will be taken up by policymakers, government officials, institutional economists, intelligence experts. The distinction between "humanists" and persons whose work has policy implications, or political significance, can be broadened further by saying that the former's ideological color is a matter of incidental importance to politics, whereas the ideology of the latter is woven directly into his material—indeed, economics, politics, and sociology in the modern academy are ideological sciences—and therefore taken for granted as being "political."

Nevertheless, the determining impingement on most knowledge produced in the contemporary West is that it be nonpolitical, that is, scholarly, academic, impartial, above partisan or small-minded doctrinal belief. One can have no quarrel with such an ambition in theory, perhaps, but in practice the reality is much more problematic. No one has ever devised a method for detaching the scholar from the circumstances of life, from the fact of his involvement (conscious or unconscious) with a class, a set of beliefs, a social position, or from the mere activity of being a member of a society. These continue to bear on what he does professionally, even though naturally enough his research and its fruits do attempt to reach a level of relative freedom from the inhibitions and the restrictions of brute, everyday reality. For there is such a thing as knowledge that is less, rather than more, partial than the individual (with his entangling and distracting life circumstances) who produces it. Yet this knowledge is not therefore automatically ____②____.

What is the writer's opinion about the argument expressed in the underlined words in ①? Do not copy more than SIX consecutive words from the passage. Second, fill in the blank with the ONE most appropriate word from the passage.

NOTE

Step 1	**S**urvey
Key Words	
Signal Words	
Step 2	**R**eading
Purpose	
Pattern of Organization	
Tone	
Main Idea	
Step 3	**S**ummary
지문 요약하기 (Paraphrasing)	
Step 4	**R**ecite
	요약문 말로 설명하기

MEMO

21 Read the passage and follow the directions. [4 points]

> Love of money has been denounced by moralists since the world began. I do not wish to add another to the moral denunciations, of which the efficacy in the past has not been encouraging. I wish to show how the worship of money is both an effect and a cause of diminishing vitality and how our institutions might be changed so as to make the worship of money grow less and the general vitality grow more. It is not the desire for money as a means to definite ends that is in question. A struggling artist may desire money in order to have leisure for his art, but this desire is finite and can be satisfied fully by a very modest sum. It is the worship of money that I wish to consider: the belief that all values may be measured in terms of money, and that money is the ultimate test of success in life. This belief is held in fact, if not in words, by multitudes of men and women, and yet it is not in harmony with human nature, since it ignores vital needs and the instinctive tendency towards some specific kind of growth. It makes men treat as unimportant those of their desires which run counter to the acquisition of money, and yet such desires are, as a rule, more important to well-being than any increase of income. It leads men to mutilate their own natures from a mistaken theory of what constitutes success, and to admire enterprises that add nothing to human welfare. It promotes a dead uniformity of character and purpose, a diminution in the joy of life, and a stress and strain which leaves whole communities weary, discouraged, and disillusioned.

Describe the writer's opinion about the moralists' denunciations. Second, identify what the worship of money disregards.

_____
_____
_____
_____
_____

NOTE

Step 1	**S**urvey
Key Words	
Signal Words	
Step 2	**R**eading
Purpose	
Pattern of Organization	
Tone	
Main Idea	
Step 3	**S**ummary
지문 요약하기 (Paraphrasing)	
Step 4	**R**ecite
	요약문 말로 설명하기

22 Read the passage and follow the directions. [4 points]

> Sometimes such innovators are of a sombre sincerity, like Tolstoi, sometimes of a sensitive and feminine eloquence, like Nietzsche. In those cases they make a stir and perhaps found a school. It is always supposed that the man in question has discovered a new idea, but, ① <u>in fact what is new is not the idea, but only the isolation of the idea</u>.
>
> In case this point is not clear, I will take one example, in reference to notions fashionable among some of the more fanciful and younger theorists. Nietzsche, as everyone knows, preached a doctrine which he and his followers regard apparently as very revolutionary: he held that ordinary altruistic morality had been the invention of a slave class to prevent the emergence of superior types to fight and rule them. Now, modern people, whether they agree with this or not, always talk of it as a new and unheard-of idea. It is calmly and persistently supposed that the great writers of the past, say Shakespeare for instance, did not hold this view, because they had never imagined it, because it had never come into their heads. Turn to the last act of Shakespeare's *Richard III* and you will find not only all that Nietzsche had to say put into two lines, but you will find it put in the very words of Nietzsche. Richard Crookback says to his nobles: *Conscience is but a word that cowards use,/ Devised at first to keep the strong in awe.*
>
> As I have said, the fact is plain. Shakespeare had thought of Nietzsche and the master morality, but he weighed it at its proper value and put it in its proper place. Its proper place is the mouth of a half-insane hunchback on the eve of defeat. This rage against the weak is only possible in a man morbidly brave but fundamentally sick: a man like Richard, a man like Nietzsche. This case alone ought to destroy the absurd fancy that these modern philosophies are modern in the sense that the great men of the past did not think of them. They thought of them; only they did not think much of them. It was not that Shakespeare did not see the Nietzsche idea; ② <u>he saw it, and he saw through it</u>.

Explain what the underlined "in fact what is new is not the idea, but only the isolation of the idea" means. Second, explain what the underlined "he saw it, and he saw through it" means.

___

NOTE

Step 1	**S**urvey
Key Words	
Signal Words	
Step 2	**R**eading
Purpose	
Pattern of Organization	
Tone	
Main Idea	
Step 3	**S**ummary
지문 요약하기 (Paraphrasing)	
Step 4	**R**ecite
	요약문 말로 설명하기

23 Read the passage and follow the directions. [4 points]

　　Here is one widely-regarded reason to worry about the growing inequality of American life: Too great a gap between rich and poor undermines the solidarity that democratic citizenship requires. Here's how: as inequality deepens, rich and poor live increasingly separate lives. The affluent send their children to private schools (or to public schools in wealthy suburbs), leaving urban public schools to the children of families who have no alternative. A similar trend leads to the secession by the privileged from other public institutions and facilities. Private health clubs replace municipal recreation centers and swimming pools. Upscale residential communities hire private security guards and rely less on public police protection. A second or third car removes the need to rely on public transportation. And so on. The affluent secede from public places and services, leaving them to those who can't afford anything else.

　　This has two bad effects, one fiscal, the other civic. First, public services deteriorate, as those who no longer use those services become less willing to support them with their taxes. Second, public institutions such as schools, parks, playgrounds, and community centers cease to be places where citizens from different walks of life encounter one another. Institutions that once gathered people together and served as informal schools of civic virtue become few and far between. The hollowing out of the public realm makes it difficult to cultivate the solidarity and sense of community on which democratic citizenship depends.

　　If the erosion of the public realm is the problem, what is the solution? A politics of the common good would take as one of its primary goals the reconstruction of the infrastructure of civic life. Rather than focus on redistribution for the sake of broadening access to private consumption, it would tax the affluent to rebuild public institutions and services so that rich and poor alike would want to take advantage of them.

An earlier generation made a massive investment in the federal highway program, which gave Americans unprecedented individual mobility and freedom, but also contributed to the reliance on the private automobile, suburban sprawl, environmental degradation, and living patterns corrosive to community. This generation could commit itself to an equally consequential investment in an infrastructure for civic renewal: public schools to which rich and poor alike would want to send their children; public transportation systems reliable enough to attract upscale commuters; and public health clinics, playgrounds, parks, recreation centers, libraries, and museums that would, ideally at least, draw people out of their gated communities and into the common spaces of a shared democratic citizenship.

Identify the negative effects of the diminution of public institutions. Second, describe the specific solution to the erosion of the public realm proffered by the writer.

NOTE

Step 1	Survey
Key Words	
Signal Words	
Step 2	**Reading**
Purpose	
Pattern of Organization	
Tone	
Main Idea	
Step 3	**Summary**
지문 요약하기 (Paraphrasing)	
Step 4	**Recite**
	요약문 말로 설명하기

MEMO

24 Read the passage and follow the directions. [4 points]

> When he graduated from university with a degree in ethnic studies, Anthony found a solid job in his profession, married, and had two sons, Sammy and Tony. Twelve years later, he moved to another company that promised steady advancement within its managerial ranks. A devoted family man, he admired his wife Lauren's dedication to raising the boys. But he also observed that his sons, approaching their teen years, benefited greatly from his fatherly friendship and counsel—especially as they approached what he and his wife realized could prove to be a difficult transitional period in their upbringing. So he made a commitment to spend plenty of time with them, playing baseball and helping with their schoolwork.
>
> But he also loved his work and did well at it, and it quickly became apparent that, to advance rapidly up the _____, he needed a master's degree. A nearby university offered the degree in an attractive evening-and-weekend program that would allow him to continue full-time employment. But it would soak up the next several years of his life and throw most of the family activities into his wife's hands. Anthony's dilemma set the short-term goals against the long-term ones. It was right, he felt, to honor his family's short-term needs to take care of his sons. Yet it was right to build for the long-term needs of his family.

Explain both the short-term needs and the long-term needs of Anthony's family in your own words. Do not copy more than FIVE consecutive words from the passage. Second, fill in the blank with the TWO consecutive words from the passage.

NOTE

Step 1	Survey
Key Words	
Signal Words	
Step 2	**Reading**
Purpose	
Pattern of Organization	
Tone	
Main Idea	
Step 3	**Summary**
지문 요약하기 (Paraphrasing)	
Step 4	**Recite**
	요약문 말로 설명하기

25 Read the passage and follow the directions. [4 points]

Zoos were originally created as places of entertainment, and their suggested involvement with conservation didn't seriously arise until about 40 years ago, when the Zoological Society of London held the first formal international meeting on the subject. Eight years later, a series of world conferences took place, entitled "The Breeding of Endangered Species," and from this point onwards conservation became the zoo community's buzzword. This commitment has now been clearly defined in The World Zoo Conservation Strategy (WZCS). However, the important and welcome document is based on an unrealistic optimism about the nature of the zoo industry.

The WZCS estimates that there are about 10,000 zoos in the world, of which around 1,000 represent a core of quality collections capable of participating in co-ordinated conservation programmes. This is the document's first failing, as I believe that 10,000 is a serious underestimate of the total number of places masquerading as zoological establishments. Of course it is difficult to get accurate data but, to put the issue into perspective, I have found that, in a year of working in Eastern Europe, I discover fresh zoos on almost a weekly basis.

The second flaw in the reasoning of the WZCS document is the naive faith it places in its 1,000 core zoos. One would assume that the calibre of these institutions would have been carefully examined, but it appears that the criterion for inclusion on this select list is that the zoo is a member of a zoo federation or association. This might be a good starting point, working on the premise that members must meet certain standards, but again the facts don't support the theory. The greatly respected American Association of Zoological Parks and Aquariums has had extremely dubious members, and the Federation of Zoological Gardens of Great Britain and Ireland has occasionally had members that have been roundly censured in the national press. These include Robin Hill Adventure Park on the Isle of Wight, which many considered the most notorious collection of animals in the country.

Identify the goal and the two defects of the WZCS document. Then, explain the reason the writer mentions Robin Hill Adventure Park. Do not copy more than FIVE consecutive words from the passage.

___

___

___

NOTE

Step 1	**S**urvey
Key Words	
Signal Words	
Step 2	**Reading**
Purpose	
Pattern of Organization	
Tone	
Main Idea	
Step 3	**Summary**
지문 요약하기 (Paraphrasing)	
Step 4	**Recite**
	요약문 말로 설명하기

26 Read the passage and follow the directions. [4 points]

> The nineteenth century suffered from a curious division between its political ideas and its economic practices. In politics it carried out the liberal ideas of Locke and Rousseau, which were adapted to a society of small peasant proprietors. Its watchwords were *liberty* and *equality*, but meanwhile it was inventing the technique which is leading the twentieth century to destroy liberty and to replace equality by new forms of oligarchy. The prevalence of liberal thought has been in some ways a misfortune, since it has prevented men of large vision from thinking out in an impersonal manner the problems raised by industrialism. Socialism and Communism, it is true, are essentially industrial creeds, but their outlook is so dominated by the class war that they have little leisure to give to anything but the means of achieving political victory. Traditional morality gives very little help in the modern world. A rich man may plunge millions into destitution by some act which not even the severest Catholic confessor would consider sinful, while he will need absolution for a trivial sexual aberration which, at the worst, has wasted an hour that might have been more usefully employed. There is need of a new doctrine on the subject of my duty to my neighbor. It is not only traditional religious teaching that fails to give adequate guidance on this subject, but also the teaching of nineteenth-century liberalism. Take, for example, Stuart Mill on liberty. Mill maintains that while the state has a right to interfere with those of my actions that have serious consequences to others, it should leave me free where the effects of my actions are mainly confined to myself. Such a principle, however, in the modern world, leaves hardly any scope for individual freedom. As society becomes more organic, the effects of men upon each other become more and more numerous and important, so that there remains hardly anything in regard to which Mill's defense of liberty is applicable.

Describe Stuart Mill's theory on liberty and explain the reason the writer considers Mill's theory to be defective. Do not copy more than SEVEN consecutive words from the passage.

NOTE

Step 1	Survey
Key Words	
Signal Words	
Step 2	**Reading**
Purpose	
Pattern of Organization	
Tone	
Main Idea	
Step 3	**Summary**
지문 요약하기 (Paraphrasing)	
Step 4	**Recite**
	요약문 말로 설명하기

27 Read the passage and follow the directions. [4 points]

One of the most infamous incidents in New York City history was the 1964 stabbing death of Kitty Genovese. She was chased by her assailant and attacked three times on the street over the course of half an hour as thirty-eight of her neighbors watched from their windows. During that time, however, none of the thirty eight witnesses called the police. The case provoked rounds of self-recrimination. Abe Rosenthal, who would later become editor of the *New York Times,* wrote that nobody can say why the thirty-eight did not pick up the phone while Miss Genovese was being attacked, since they cannot say themselves. It can be assumed, however, that their apathy was indeed one of the big-city variety. It is almost a matter of psychological survival, if one is surrounded and pressed by millions of people, to prevent them from constantly impinging on you, and the only way to do this is to ignore them as often as possible. Indifference to one's neighbor and his troubles is a conditioned reflex in life in New York as it is in other big cities. This is the kind of environmental explanation that makes intuitive sense to us. The truth about Genovese, however, turns out to be a little more complicated—and more interesting. Two psychologists—Bibb Latane of Columbia University and John Darley of New York University—subsequently conducted a series of studies to try to understand what they dubbed the "bystander problem." They staged emergencies of one kind or another in different situations in order to see who would come and help. What they found was surprising. In one experiment, for example, Latane and Darley had a student alone in a room stage an epileptic fit. When there was just one person next door, listening, that person rushed to the student's aid 85 percent of the time. But when subjects thought that there were four others also overhearing the seizure, they came to the student's aid only 31 percent of the time. In another experiment, people who saw smoke seeping out from under a doorway would report it 75 percent of the time when they were on their own, but the incident would be reported only 38 percent of the time when they were in a group. When people are in a group, in other words, responsibility for acting is diffused. They assume that someone else will make the call, or they assume that because no one else is acting, the apparent problem—the seizure-like sounds from the other room, the smoke from the door—isn't really a problem. Ironically, had she been attacked on a lonely street with just one witness, she might have lived.

What is Abe Rosenthal's explanation of the case of Kitty Genovese? Second, describe what Latane and Darley find.

NOTE

Step 1	Survey
Key Words	
Signal Words	
Step 2	**Reading**
Purpose	
Pattern of Organization	
Tone	
Main Idea	
Step 3	**Summary**
지문 요약하기 (Paraphrasing)	
Step 4	**Recite**
	요약문 말로 설명하기

MEMO

28 Read the passage and follow the directions. [4 points]

> In Cambridge in the 1920s, F. P. Ramsey single-handedly forged a range of ideas that have since come to define the philosophical landscape. Contemporary debates about truth, meaning, knowledge, logic and the structure of scientific theories all take off from positions first defined by Ramsey. A year before Ramsey died from hepatitis at the age of twenty-six in 1930, Ludwig Wittgenstein returned to Cambridge after his reclusive years in Austria. The cult surrounding Wittgenstein quickly caught fire, and for the next fifty years dominated philosophy throughout the English-speaking world. By the time it subsided, Ramsey had somehow been relegated to a minor role in history.
>
> In some ways, Ramsey and Wittgenstein had much in common. They were both inspired by Russell and saw their initial task in philosophy as improving its account of the relation between language and reality. But they had very different philosophical temperaments. Wittgenstein's first book added a powerful dose of mysticism to his analysis of language, and this gnostic strain became even more pronounced in the neo-idealism of his later philosophy. Ramsey, by contrast, saw the world through the lens of mathematics and fundamental physics. For Wittgenstein, science was an enemy; for Ramsey, it became a friend.
>
> In 1929, Wittgenstein returned to Cambridge for good. He and Ramsey made up their differences and for the best part of a year resumed philosophical discussion. But it is hard to imagine that they would have continued in intellectual harmony for long. Wittgenstein's transcendental hankerings made him impatient with what he saw as Ramsey's materialism. Ramsey for his part was irritated by Wittgenstein's exclusive focus on his own ideas. Over the past century the philosophical landscape has shifted. The central challenge is now to accommodate mind and meaning within the world uncovered by science, and _____ for some higher perspective have been marginalized. Now it is good to be reminded how far Ramsey went in meeting this challenge.

2S2R 유형

Write the ONE most appropriate word from the passage that best fills the blank. Additionally, describe what can be inferred regarding the current, relative popularity of Wittgenstein in the shifted philosophical landscape the writer outlines.

_____

_____

_____

NOTE

Step 1	**S**urvey
Key Words	
Signal Words	
Step 2	**R**eading
Purpose	
Pattern of Organization	
Tone	
Main Idea	
Step 3	**S**ummary
지문 요약하기 (Paraphrasing)	
Step 4	**R**ecite
요약문 말로 설명하기	

A형 서술형 127

29. Read the passage and follow the directions. [4 points]

Five years have passed since the onset of what is sometimes called the Great Recession. While the economy has slowly improved, there are still millions of Americans leading lives of quiet desperation: without jobs, without resources, without hope. Who was to blame? Was it simply a result of negligence, of the kind of inordinate risk-taking commonly called a "bubble," of an imprudent but innocent failure to maintain adequate reserves for a rainy day? Or was it the result, at least in part, of fraudulent practices, of dubious mortgages portrayed as sound risks and packaged into ever more esoteric financial instruments, the fundamental weaknesses of which were intentionally obscured? If it was the former, then the criminal law has no role to play in the aftermath. For in all but a few circumstances, the fierce and fiery weapon called criminal prosecution is directed at intentional fraud, and nothing less. If the Great Recession was in no part the handiwork of intentionally fraudulent practices by high-level executives, then to prosecute such executives criminally would be "scapegoating" of the most shallow and despicable kind. But if, by contrast, the Great Recession was the product of _____, the failure to prosecute those responsible must be judged one of the most egregious failures of the criminal justice system in many years. Indeed, it would stand in striking contrast to the increased success that federal prosecutors have had over the past fifty years or so in bringing to justice even the highest-level figures who orchestrated mammoth frauds.

Fill in the blank with the TWO most appropriate consecutive words from the passage. Then, explain what can be inferred regarding the success of prosecution of high-level fraud half a century earlier.

_____
_____
_____
_____

NOTE

Step 1	**S**urvey
Key Words	
Signal Words	
Step 2	**R**eading
Purpose	
Pattern of Organization	
Tone	
Main Idea	
Step 3	**S**ummary
지문 요약하기 (Paraphrasing)	
Step 4	**R**ecite
	요약문 말로 설명하기

30. Read the passage and follow the directions. [4 points]

> Cloning and the new technologies of human genetic modification are among the most powerful and consequential technologies ever developed. Two constituencies dominate the current _____ over cloning: antiabortion conservatives and biomedical scientists. Many pro-choice feminists worry about a new eugenics that would commodify the process of child-bearing. Human-rights advocates worry that new eugenic technologies would throw fuel on the flames of racial and ethnic hatred. Although both sides support bans on creating cloned children, conservatives also want immediate, permanent bans on the use of cloning techniques that might have research applications, while the biotech industry resists any meaningful regulation whatsoever. It's been suggested as a compromise that Congress enact a ban on creating cloned children while imposing a moratorium, rather than a permanent ban, on research cloning. During a moratorium, the many proposed alternatives to the use of clonal embryos for research could be explored. Unfortunately, on that debate, neither side has yet been willing to make the first public move towards pragmatic compromises of this sort. To break <u>this deadlock</u>, we need a broader range of constituencies considering the full implications of cloning.

Fill in the blank with the ONE most appropriate word from the passage. Second, describe to what the underlined part refers.

NOTE

Step 1	**S**urvey
Key Words	
Signal Words	
Step 2	**R**eading
Purpose	
Pattern of Organization	
Tone	
Main Idea	
Step 3	**S**ummary
지문 요약하기 (Paraphrasing)	
Step 4	**R**ecite

요약문 말로 설명하기

31 Read the passage and follow the directions. [4 points]

> In *The Black Swan*, Nassim Taleb introduced the notion of a narrative fallacy to describe how flawed stories of the past shape our views of the world and our expectations for the future. Narrative fallacies arise inevitably from our continuous attempt to make sense of the world. The explanatory stories that people find compelling are simple; are concrete rather than abstract; assign a larger role to talent, stupidity, and intentions than to luck; and focus on a few striking events that happened rather than on the countless events that failed to happen. Taleb suggests that we humans constantly fool ourselves by constructing flimsy accounts of the past and believing they are true. Good stories provide a simple and coherent account of people's actions and intentions. You are always ready to interpret behavior as a manifestation of general propensities and personality traits—causes that you can readily match to effects. The halo effect contributes to coherence, because it inclines us to match our view of all the qualities of a person to our judgement of one attribute that is particularly significant. The halo effect helps keep explanatory narratives simple and coherent by exaggerating the consistency of evaluations : good people do only good things and bad people are all bad. The statement "Hitler loved dogs and little children" is shocking no matter how many times you hear it, because any trace of kindness in someone so evil violates the expectations set up by the halo effect. Inconsistencies reduce the ease of our thoughts and the clarity of our feelings.

Describe what the halo effect is in one sentence. Also, what would be the feeling of the reader if a story was consistent in narrative, according to the passage?

NOTE

Step 1	**S**urvey
Key Words	
Signal Words	
Step 2	**R**eading
Purpose	
Pattern of Organization	
Tone	
Main Idea	
Step 3	**S**ummary
지문 요약하기 (Paraphrasing)	
Step 4	**R**ecite
	요약문 말로 설명하기

32 Read the passage and follow the directions. [4 points]

> The notion that geniuses such as Shakespeare, Mozart, and Picasso were "gifted" or possessed innate talents is a myth according to a study by a British psychologist. After examining outstanding performances in the arts and sports, Professor Michael Howe and colleagues at Exeter University concluded that excellence is determined by opportunities, encouragement, training, motivation, self-confidence, and—most of all—practice.
>
> The theory—a radical break with traditional beliefs—has been applauded by academics worldwide. It has significant implications for teachers and parents, not least because children who are not thought to be gifted are being denied the encouragement they need to succeed. The authors took as their starting point the "widespread belief that to reach high levels of ability a person must possess an innate potential called talent." They said it was important to establish whether the belief was correct because ① it had social and educational consequences affecting selection procedures and training.
>
> However, studies of accomplished artists and mathematicians, top tennis players and swimmers reported few early signs of promise prior to parental _____②_____. No case was found of anyone reaching the highest levels of achievement without devoting thousands of hours to serious training. Even those who were believed to be exceptionally talented—whether in music, mathematics, chess, or sports—required lengthy periods of instruction and practice.

Identify to what the underlined "it" refers. Second, fill in the blank with the ONE most appropriate word found in the passage.

NOTE

Step 1	**S**urvey
Key Words	
Signal Words	
Step 2	**R**eading
Purpose	
Pattern of Organization	
Tone	
Main Idea	
Step 3	**S**ummary
지문 요약하기 (Paraphrasing)	
Step 4	**R**ecite
	요약문 말로 설명하기

33 Read the passage and follow the directions. [4 points]

> After learning a new physical skill, such as riding a bike, it takes six hours to permanently store the memory in the brain. But interrupt the storage process by learning another new skill and that first lesson may be erased, according to research into memory and the mind. "We've shown that time itself is a very powerful component of learning," said Dr. Henry Holcomb, a psychiatrist who heads a Johns Hopkins University group that studies how people remember. "It is not enough to simply practice something. You have to allow time to pass for the brain to encode the new skill." The researchers used a device that measures blood flow in the brain. They concluded it takes five to six hours for the memory of a new skill to move from a temporary storage site in the front of the brain to a permanent storage site at the back. During those six hours, Holcomb said, there is a neural "window of vulnerability" when that _____ can be easily eroded from memory if the person attempts to learn a second new skill. "If you were performing a piano piece for the first time and then immediately started practicing something else, then that will cause problems in retention of the initial piece that you practiced," Holcomb said. It would be better, he said, if the first practice session were followed by five to six hours of <u>routine activity</u> that required no new learning.

Fill in the blank with the TWO most appropriate consecutive words from the passage. Second, explain the implied important characteristic of the "routine activity" described in the final sentence.

_____
_____
_____
_____
_____

NOTE

Step 1	**S**urvey
Key Words	
Signal Words	
Step 2	**R**eading
Purpose	
Pattern of Organization	
Tone	
Main Idea	
Step 3	**S**ummary
지문 요약하기 (Paraphrasing)	
Step 4	**R**ecite
	요약문 말로 설명하기

34 Read the passage and follow the directions. [4 points]

> The separation of space inside homes may vary from culture to culture. In most American homes the layout of rooms reveals the separateness and labeling of space according to _____ —bedroom, living room, dining room, playroom, and so on. This system is in sharp contrast to other cultures where one room in a house may serve several functions. In Japan, homes with sliding walls can change a large room into two small rooms so that a living room can also serve as a bedroom. When a home or a city's design is influenced by another culture, the "native" architecture can be lost or disguised. For example, a French architect was asked to design Chandigarh, the capital city in Punjab, India. He decided to plan the city with centralized shopping centers which required public transportation and movement away from the village centers. Eventually the Indians stopped meeting each other socially in their small neighborhoods. Apparently, the introduction of a non-Indian style of architecture affected some of the cultural and social patterns of those living in the city.

Fill in the blank with the ONE most appropriate word from the passage. Second, explain what type of marketplaces we can infer that Chandigarh had previous to its redesign.

_____
_____
_____
_____
_____

NOTE

Step 1	**S**urvey
Key Words	
Signal Words	
Step 2	**R**eading
Purpose	
Pattern of Organization	
Tone	
Main Idea	
Step 3	**S**ummary
지문 요약하기 (Paraphrasing)	
Step 4	**R**ecite
	요약문 말로 설명하기

35 **Read the passage and follow the directions.** [4 points]

> The wolf prowls through stories as the embodiment of evil. In a way, it is odd that the wolf should be mankind's worst enemy. Bears, which get a far better press, are more dangerous. Disturb a bear and it may turn on you; disturb a wolf and it will run away. Presumably competition explains this ancient hatred. A pack of wolves will happily kill hundreds of sheep in an hour. <u>In communities whose livelihood goes about on four legs, wolves and people are not compatible</u>. This rivalry spawned awful cruelty, and in the early 19th century America, killing wolves was regarded as fine entertainment. Yet around the middle of the 20th century sentiment started to change. First came a shift in conservationist thinking, illustrated by the life and writings of Aldo Leopold, father of the American environmental movement. In the early 20th century environmentalists believed that because predators killed other animals, conservation was best served by killing them. But Mr Leopold righteously grew concerned about the consequences of this campaign. In one of his best-selling environmentalist books, he wrote, "I have watched the face of many a newly wolfless mountain, and seen the south-facing slopes wrinkle with a maze of new deer trails. I have seen every edible bush and seedling browsed, first to anaemic desuetude, and then to death."

Elucidate the meaning of the underlined words. Then, describe the writer's opinion of wolves in ONE sentence.

_____
_____
_____
_____

NOTE

Step 1	**S**urvey
Key Words	
Signal Words	
Step 2	**R**eading
Purpose	
Pattern of Organization	
Tone	
Main Idea	
Step 3	**S**ummary
지문 요약하기 (Paraphrasing)	
Step 4	**R**ecite
	요약문 말로 설명하기

36 Read the passage and follow the directions. [4 points]

> For nearly a century, surgical residency had been a period of both intensive experience and increasing responsibility. More recent research has affirmed that approach, demonstrating the strong link between a surgeon's operative skill, the number of operations performed and patient outcomes. For the past decade, with limits set on their time at the hospital, young surgeons-in-training had fewer opportunities to scrub in on operations. While previous generations of trainees participated in at least one operation a day, new trainees had only enough time to be involved in two or maybe three operations each week. Calculating the number of hours "lost" by cutting back on in-hospital time, surgical leaders estimated that young surgeons-to-be were now missing out on as much as a year's worth of experience. Surgery itself was also changing, and the number of skills surgeons now needed was expanding. The discovery of new medications rendered once standard operations less common, but not entirely obsolete; so surgeons still had to know how to perform all the operations without getting to practice them as often. Surgical training programs scrambled to make up for less time and cover the ever-expanding body of knowledge by creating online educational tools and offering trainees experiences in simulated operating rooms and trauma resuscitations using electronic mannequins. But as a study reveals, even the best-equipped simulation labs cannot replace a year's worth of lost experience.

Explain the writer's main purpose for writing the passage. Additionally, according to the writer, how often should a surgeon in a residency participate in an operation to be trained best?

_____

_____

_____

_____

NOTE

Step 1	Surhvey
Key Words	
Signal Words	
Step 2	**Reading**
Purpose	
Pattern of Organization	
Tone	
Main Idea	
Step 3	**Summary**
지문 요약하기 (Paraphrasing)	
Step 4	**Recite**
	요약문 말로 설명하기

37 Read the passage and follow the directions. [4 points]

> The broadcast and print media regularly provide hype for individuals who have achieved "super" success. These stories are usually about celebrities and superstars from the sports and entertainment world. Society pages and gossip columns serve to keep the social elite informed of each other's doings, allow the rest of us to gawk at their excesses, and help to keep the American dream alive. The print media are also fond of feature stories on corporate empire builders. These stories provide an occasional "insider's" view of the private and corporate life of industrialists by suggesting a "rags to riches" account of corporate success. These stories tell us that corporate success is a series of smart moves, shrewd acquisitions, timely mergers, and well-thought-out executive suite shuffles. By painting the upper class in a positive light, innocent of any wrongdoing (labor leaders and union organizations usually get the opposite treatment), the _____ assure us that wealth and power are benevolent. One person's capital accumulation is presumed to be good for all. The elite, then, are portrayed as investment wizards, people of special talent and skill, whom even their victims (workers and consumers) can admire.

What is the writer's purpose in the passage? Write your answer in about 10 words. Second, fill in the blank with the ONE most appropriate word from the passage.

_____

_____

_____

_____

NOTE

Step 1	**S**urvey
Key Words	
Signal Words	
Step 2	**R**eading
Purpose	
Pattern of Organization	
Tone	
Main Idea	
Step 3	**S**ummary
지문 요약하기 (Paraphrasing)	
Step 4	**R**ecite
	요약문 말로 설명하기

38 Read the passage and follow the directions. [4 points]

To begin with, all the standard arguments about why the brain might not be a computer are pretty weak. Take the argument that "brains are parallel, but computers are serial." Critics are right to note that virtually every time a human does anything, many different parts of the brain are engaged; that's parallel, not serial.

But the idea that computers are strictly serial is woefully out of date. Ever since desktop computers became popular, there has always been some degree of parallelism in computers, with several different computations being performed simultaneously, by different components, such as the hard-drive controller and the central processor. And the trend over time in the hardware business has been to make computers more and more parallel, using new approaches like multicore processors and graphics processing units.

Skeptics of the computer metaphor also like to argue that "brains are analog, while computers are digital." The idea here is that things that are digital operate only with discrete divisions, as with a digital watch; things that are analog, like an old-fashioned watch, work on a smooth continuum.

But just as either format is possible for a watch, either format is possible for a(n) _____, and many "digital" computer switches are built out of analog components and processes. Although virtually all modern computers are digital, most early computers were analog. And we still don't really know whether our brains are analog or digital or some mix of the two.

Also, there is a popular argument that human brains are capable of generating emotions, whereas computers are not. But while computers as we know them clearly lack emotions, that fact itself doesn't mean that emotions aren't the product of computation. On the contrary, neural systems like the amygdala that modulate emotions appear to work in roughly the same way as the rest of the brain does, which is to say that they transmit signals and integrate information, and transform inputs into outputs. As any computer scientist will tell you, that's pretty much what computers do.

In the passage, there are three sorts of skeptics, whom the writer of the passage argues against. What are those skeptics' ideas and what does the writer argue against them? Do NOT copy more than FIVE consecutive words from the passage. Second, fill in the blank with the ONE most appropriate word from the passage.

___

___

___

NOTE

Step 1	**S**urvey
Key Words	
Signal Words	
Step 2	**R**eading
Purpose	
Pattern of Organization	
Tone	
Main Idea	
Step 3	**S**ummary
지문 요약하기 (Paraphrasing)	
Step 4	**R**ecite
	요약문 말로 설명하기

39 Read the passage and follow the directions. [4 points]

> We all have our favourite movie moments, ones we love to watch again from time to time. Chimpanzees and bonobos, too, have the nous to recall thrilling scenes in movies they have previously seen and anticipate when they are about to come up. Apes can readily recall and anticipate significant recent events, just by watching those events once. Rather than use hidden food as a memory test, Japanese researchers made short movies and showed them to apes on two consecutive days.
>
> Kano and his colleague Satoshi Hirata made and starred in two short films. Another of the characters was a human dressed up as an ape in a King Kong costume who carried out attacks on people, providing the key plot moment in the first movie. Both films were designed to contain memorable dramatic events, and the researchers deployed laser eye-tracking technology to see if the animals preferentially noticed and remembered these moments.
>
> The researchers hoped that enacting an emotionally charged scene involving aggression would help them tease out any inklings of memory. In the first of the two 30-second-long movies, the ape character bursts in through the door on the right—one of two visible on screen—and attacks one of the two people 18 seconds in.
>
> Through tracking the gaze of six chimpanzees and six bonobos, the researchers found that on a second viewing, the animals preferentially looked at the right-hand doorway around 3 seconds before the ape burst in, demonstrating recall of locational content. The second movie allowed them to show that the apes could also remember what items were relevant to a plot.
>
> In the first screening, a human character chose one of two adjacent weapons to launch a revenge attack on the ape 24 seconds in. Cunningly, the second screening used a slightly different version which swapped the positions of the two weapons. The animals focused their anticipatory glances on the weapon used in the first showing, not where it had been in the first showing, demonstrating that they knew what it would be used for and their expectation that the character would select it again, even though it was in a different place.

Explain what the Japanese researchers found in their experiment about apes and what the difference between their method and previous method is. When you answer the questions, do NOT copy more than FIVE consecutive words from the passage.

_____

_____

_____

NOTE

Step 1	**S**urvey
Key Words	
Signal Words	
Step 2	**R**eading
Purpose	
Pattern of Organization	
Tone	
Main Idea	
Step 3	**S**ummary
지문 요약하기 (Paraphrasing)	
Step 4	**R**ecite
	요약문 말로 설명하기

40 Read the passage and follow the directions. [4 points]

> To one who stands outside the cycle of beliefs and passions which make the war seem necessary, an isolation, an almost unbearable separation from the general activity, becomes unavoidable. At the very moment when the universal disaster raises compassion in the highest degree, compassion itself compels aloofness from the impulse to self-destruction which has swept over the world. The helpless longing to save men from the ruin towards which they are hastening makes it necessary to oppose the stream, to incur hostility, to be thought unfeeling, to lose for the moment the power of winning belief. It is impossible to prevent others from feeling hostile, but it is possible to avoid any reciprocal _____ on one's own part, by imaginative understanding and the sympathy which grows out of it. And without understanding and sympathy it is impossible to find a cure for the evil from which the world is suffering.
>
> There are two views of the war neither of which seems to me adequate. The usual view in this country is that it is due to the wickedness of the Germans; the view of most pacifists is that it is due to the diplomatic tangle and to the ambitions of Governments. I think both these views fail to realize the extent to which war grows out of ordinary human nature. Germans, and also the men who compose Governments, are on the whole average human beings, actuated by the same passions that actuate others, not differing much from the rest of the world except in their circumstances. War is accepted by men who are neither Germans nor diplomatists with a readiness, an acquiescence in untrue and inadequate reasons, which would not be possible if any deep repugnance to war were widespread in other nations or classes. The untrue things which men believe, and the true things which they disbelieve, are an index to their impulses—not necessarily to individual impulses in each case (since beliefs are contagious), but to the general impulses of the community.

Fill in the blank with the ONE most appropriate word from the passage. If necessary, change the word form. Second, describe the two conventional opinions on the war and explain why the writer does not accept those views. When you answer the questions, do NOT copy more than FIVE consecutive words from the passage.

2S2R 유형

NOTE

Step 1	**S**urvey
Key Words	
Signal Words	
Step 2	**R**eading
Purpose	
Pattern of Organization	
Tone	
Main Idea	
Step 3	**S**ummary
지문 요약하기 (Paraphrasing)	
Step 4	**R**ecite
	요약문 말로 설명하기

A형 서술형 151

41 Read the passage and follow the directions. [4 points]

> Miles Davis was a ① <u>protean</u> figure in Jazz; like some musical Picasso, he mastered and then shed a series of styles throughout the course of his career. This is rare in any artist, but almost unheard of in the world of jazz, where a musician's style is usually formed extremely early, and then refined and repeated for the remainder of his or her life. Although Davis could have earned millions by continuing to play the music that had first made him famous in the 1950s, he refused to repeat himself. He consistently sought to expand his musical horizon, working with young, emerging musicians, restlessly searching for new sounds.
>
> After cutting his teeth on the bebop jazz of the 1940s, David developed a "cooker" style and made his name in the 1950s with a five-man combo. The so-called "purists" have often claimed that ② <u>this period represents the zenith of Davis's achievement</u>. But this argument reveals more about the narrow tastes of certain critics than it does about the supposed limitations of Miles Davis. The groups Davis led in the 1960s featured a new generation of superb musicians such as Wayne Shorter and Herbie Hancok, and produced music that explored new and complex rhythmic textures.
>
> Yet critics continued to complain. And when Davis released Bitches Brew in 1970, the jazz "purists" were horrified: His band was using electronic instruments, and its music borrowed heavily from rock rhythms and the psychedelic sound of "acid" rock. Typically, Davis ignored the storm of protest, secure in his artistic vision. Throughout the early 1970s, he continued to attract the best new players to his side. They benefited from his vast experience and mastery, and he from their youthful energy and fresh approach to the music.

According to the passage, what is the difference between Miles Davis and most jazz musicians? When you answer, you may refer to the word "protean." Second, what is the writer's take on the validity of the purists' argument "this period represents the zenith of Davis's achievement"? Write your answer in about 20 words.

NOTE

Step 1	Survey
Key Words	
Signal Words	
Step 2	**Reading**
Purpose	
Pattern of Organization	
Tone	
Main Idea	
Step 3	**Summary**
지문 요약하기 (Paraphrasing)	
Step 4	**Recite**
	요약문 말로 설명하기

42 **Read the passage and follow the directions.** [4 points]

> How often have you called someone by a wrong name or title? Perhaps you were having a conference with your teacher and accidentally called him "Dad." All of us make these kinds of errors, and some of them get us into serious trouble! Research shows that we tend to confuse two people when we have similar relationships to both people. This explains why you may call your teacher "Dad", because both of them are male authority figures. This can also explain another common error, calling a boyfriend or girlfriend by the previous boyfriend or girlfriend's name. A supportive and intimate relationship with one person becomes momentarily mixed up with a supportive, warm, and intimate relationship with another. In contrast, people rarely make errors involving a very different type of _____. For instance, you are unlikely to call your professor by your ex-boyfriend's name, unless perhaps you are involved in a heated intellectual argument with the professor, and heated intellectual arguments were the mainstay of your relationship with your past boyfriend. The above finding suggests that the cognitive structure of our social relations and the perceptions we hold of other people are organized in memory not only in terms of those specific individuals, but also in terms of the nature of our social relationships with them.

Fill in the blank with the ONE most appropriate word from the passage. Second, explain the circumstances that are prerequisite for a given person to be incorrectly addressed, according to the research above.

_____

_____

_____

_____

_____

NOTE

Step 1	**S**urvey
Key Words	
Signal Words	
Step 2	**R**eading
Purpose	
Pattern of Organization	
Tone	
Main Idea	
Step 3	**S**ummary
지문 요약하기 (Paraphrasing)	
Step 4	**R**ecite
	요약문 말로 설명하기

43   Read the passage and follow the directions. [4 points]

> Bighorns are descended from wild Siberian sheep that crossed the Bering land bridge to North America about 100,000 years ago. These herds spread southward, diversifying and adapting to local habitats. Bighorn sheep inhabit steep, barren terrain that few other species can tolerate. Thanks to their hardiness, Bighorn sheep have long been a symbolic species. Early Native Americans carved their likenesses into rocks, and the first settlers embraced them as symbols of the rugged wilderness of the American West. At their peak, more than two million bighorns roamed the West, gracefully cavorting on rocky hillsides from California to Nebraska. But by the late 19th century, bighorn sheep were in trouble. The domestic sheep industry had taken hold in the West, and wild sheep had no immunity against diseases introduced by European livestock. As millions of domestic sheep inundated the landscape, deadly pathogens such as pneumonia decimated the bighorn population. Unregulated hunting took a toll on the few wild herds that remained. By 1940, the bighorn population had plummeted to fewer than 20,000, isolated in tiny enclaves scattered across the Western states. In recent decades, state wildlife management agencies have undertaken extensive conservation work to help bring bighorn sheep back from the brink. Much of the work focuses on capturing bighorns from successful herds and relocating them to other areas. The bighorns are carried in bags beneath the helicopter to a handling area where veterinarians examine the sheep for signs of _____. If the sheep are healthy, they are transported to their new home. So far, more than 2,000 sheep have been successfully transplanted. This type of intensive conservation work has helped increase Nevada's bighorn population to more than 11,000, from a low of 2,000 in the mid-20th century.

Fill in the blank above with the ONE most appropriate word found in the passage, you may change the word form if necessary. Additionally, explain the significance the Bighorn sheep had for earlier settlers and the reason for this.

NOTE

Step 1	**S**urvey
Key Words	
Signal Words	
Step 2	**R**eading
Purpose	
Pattern of Organization	
Tone	
Main Idea	
Step 3	**S**ummary
지문 요약하기 (Paraphrasing)	
Step 4	**R**ecite
	요약문 말로 설명하기

44 Read the passage and follow the directions. [4 points]

> Some facts contradict the central dogma's cardinal maxim: that a DNA gene exclusively governs the molecular processes that give rise to a particular inherited trait. Because of their commitment to an obsolete theory, most molecular biologists operate under the assumption that DNA is the secret of life, whereas the careful observation of the hierarchy of living processes strongly suggests it is the other way around.
>
> Why, then, has the _____ continued to stand? To some degree the theory has been protected from criticism by a device more common to religion than science: dissent, or merely the discovery of a discordant fact, is a punishable offense, a heresy that might easily lead to professional ostracism. Much of this bias can be attributed to institutional inertia, a failure of rigor, but there are other, more insidious, reasons why molecular geneticists might be satisfied with the status quo: the central dogma has given them such a satisfying, seductively simplistic explanation of heredity.

Fill in the blank with the TWO most appropriate consecutive words from the passage. Second, what is the protection of the status quo mentioned in the passage compared to?

_____
_____
_____
_____
_____

NOTE

Step 1	Survey
Key Words	
Signal Words	
Step 2	**Reading**
Purpose	
Pattern of Organization	
Tone	
Main Idea	
Step 3	**Summary**
지문 요약하기 (Paraphrasing)	
Step 4	**Recite**
	요약문 말로 설명하기

45 Read the passage and follow the directions. [4 points]

> Since the middle of the 20th century, a significant alteration has occurred in the relativity of conduct and moral. Before that, people had little doubt that there existed a gap between 'good' and 'bad', the former being coloured a dazzling white and the latter being coloured in unrelieved black. Freud and Jung and their disciples have changed all that, though. We now have learnt that nothing a person ever does is really his fault, but due to repressions and inhibitions derived from parental incompetence or undeveloped opportunities and glands.
>
> There are some old-fashioned people like me, however, who still regard with some distrust these explanations of psycho-analysis. Being an individualist by conviction, I regard individuals as responsible for their own actions, and the relativity of _____ responsibility inculcated by the teachings of the psycho-analyst seems to me as depressing and discouraging as the old doctrine of predestination.

In the given passage, fill in the blank with the ONE most appropriate word found in the passage. If necessary, change the word form. Then, state the author's opinion regarding Freud and Jung's point of view.

_____
_____
_____
_____
_____

NOTE

Step 1	**S**urvey
Key Words	
Signal Words	
Step 2	**R**eading
Purpose	
Pattern of Organization	
Tone	
Main Idea	
Step 3	**S**ummary
지문 요약하기 (Paraphrasing)	
Step 4	**R**ecite
	요약문 말로 설명하기

46 Read the passage and follow the directions. [4 points]

> The Civil War represents a sort of watershed in American art. At the beginning of the rebellion, romantic images still dominated painting in general as well as battle art. During the war, however, photography and illustrated journalism emerged and placed more realistic images of war before the public at low prices. Mass-produced woodcut engravings, particularly in magazines such as Harper's and Frank Leslie's *Illustrated Newspaper*, carried drawings and sketches to large audiences. While illustrated journalism flourished during the Civil War, photography was still in its infancy. Roger Fenton, an Englishman, had pioneered war photography during the Crimean War only a few years before the firing on Fort Sumter. Several practitioners followed the troops during the Civil War, most notably Mathew Brady, perhaps the best known of all American photographers. By the end of the century, photography was well on its way to displacing hand-drawn art as the basic pictorial record of war. This emergence of war photography gave painters more latitude in selection and interpretation of subjects. They were no longer compelled to commemorate important events and turned instead to narrative painting of camp life and unfamiliar skirmishes. But the shift from memorialization of critical episodes did not mean that military art became less consequential. Freed from the necessity of depicting the sweep of major events, artists could probe more deeply the emotions and strains of combat life. The resultant _____ did not draw its significance from the renown of the events portrayed but rather from what it said about men at war.

Fill in the blank with the TWO most appropriate consecutive words from the passage. Second, identify the media through which the public regarded the Civil War.

NOTE

Step 1	**S**urvey
Key Words	
Signal Words	
Step 2	**R**eading
Purpose	
Pattern of Organization	
Tone	
Main Idea	
Step 3	**S**ummary
지문 요약하기 (Paraphrasing)	
Step 4	**R**ecite
	요약문 말로 설명하기

47 Read the passage and follow the directions. [4 points]

> Why does Shylock, a Jewish loan shark in Shakespeare's play *The Merchant of Venice* turn out to be such a villain, demanding literally a pound of flesh—in effect Antonio's death—if he cannot fulfil his obligations? The answer is that Shylock is one of the many moneylenders in history to have belonged to an ethnic minority. By Shakespeare's time, Jews had been providing commercial credit in Venice for nearly a century. They did their business in front of the building once known as the Banco Rosso, which was located in a cramped ghetto some distance from the center of the city. There was a good reason why Venetian merchants had to come to the Jewish ghetto if they wanted to borrow money. For Christians, usury was a sin. Usurers had been excommunicated by the Third Lateran Council in 1179. Jews, too, were not supposed to lend at interest. But there was a convenient get-out clause in the Old Testament Book of Deuteronomy: "Unto a stranger thou mayest lend upon usury; but unto thy brother thou shalt not lend upon usury." In other words, a Jew might legitimately lend to a Christian, though not to another Jew. The price of doing so was social exclusion. In 1516, the Venetian authorities designated a special area of the city for Jews on the site of an old iron foundry which became known as the ghetto nuovo (ghetto literally means casting). There they were to be confined every night and on Christian holidays.

Based on the given passage, provide one way a Christian might loan to another legitimately.

_____
_____
_____
_____

NOTE

Step 1	**S**urvey
Key Words	
Signal Words	
Step 2	**R**eading
Purpose	
Pattern of Organization	
Tone	
Main Idea	
Step 3	**S**ummary
지문 요약하기 (Paraphrasing)	
Step 4	**R**ecite
	요약문 말로 설명하기

48   Read the passage and follow the directions. [4 points]

> Homo sapiens sapiens reached the Americas much later than they did any other landmass. The earliest confirmed human occupation in the Western Hemisphere dates to about 10,500 B.C., some forty thousand years after the settling of the Eurasian landmass and Australia. Accordingly, all human remains found so far in the Americas belong to the Homo sapiens species. We know, however, much less about the settlement of the Americas than we do about the other continents. Scholars are not certain which routes the early settlers took, when they came, or if they traveled over land or by water. Far fewer human burials have been found in the Americas, and the few that have been found were excavated with much less scientific care than in Eurasia and Africa. Many sites had been disturbed so that the original layers of earth, so valuable to archaeologists, are no longer intact. Many early sites contain no human remains at all. One theory is that humans reached America on a land bridge from Siberia. Beringia is the landmass, now below water, that connected the tip of Siberia in Russia with the northeastern corner of Alaska. Today Beringia is covered by an 80-km-wide stretch of the Bering Sea. The water in this part of the Bering Sea is shallow. As the earth experienced different periods of extended coldness, called Ice Ages, ocean water froze and covered such northern landmasses with ice. During these periods the ocean level declined and the ancient Beringia landmass emerged to form a land bridge between Russia and America.

Identify the key evidence needed to expand scholars' understanding of early human settlers of the Americas. Second, describe the problem that has occurred with gathering this key evidence so far in America.

_____
_____
_____
_____

NOTE

Step 1	**S**urvey
Key Words	
Signal Words	
Step 2	**R**eading
Purpose	
Pattern of Organization	
Tone	
Main Idea	
Step 3	**S**ummary
지문 요약하기 (Paraphrasing)	
Step 4	**R**ecite
	요약문 말로 설명하기

49   Read the passage and follow the directions. [4 points]

> Schooling is primarily a linguistic process, and language serves as an often unconscious means of evaluating and differentiating students. Inasmuch as content and disciplinary knowledge are constituted and presented through language, learning an academic subject means reading and writing texts that are organized linguistically to accomplish particular communicative purposes. In school, students are expected to use language to demonstrate what they have learned and what they think in ways that can be shared, evaluated, and further challenged or supported. But language patterns themselves are rarely the focus of attention of students and teachers. Their attention is typically on the content of the texts they read and respond to but not on the ways language construes that content. In addition, teachers' expectations for language use are seldom made explicit, and much of what is expected regarding language use in school tasks remains couched in teachers' vague admonitions to "use your own words" or to "be clear." Writing tasks are assigned without clear guidelines for students about how a particular text type is typically structured and organized. For these reasons Christie has called language the "hidden curriculum" of schooling. Judgments about students' abilities are often based on how they express their knowledge in language. The testing, counseling, and classroom interactions that inform these judgments perpetuate and maintain values that are often not made explicit. This suggests that a careful analysis of the _____ challenges of learning is important for understanding the difficulties students face and the limitations they demonstrate in talking and writing about topics they have studied.

Choose the ONE most appropriate word that best fills in the blank. Then, based on the above passage, describe the standards that teachers have that are not made explicit.

_____
_____
_____
_____

NOTE

Step 1	**S**urvey
Key Words	
Signal Words	
Step 2	**R**eading
Purpose	
Pattern of Organization	
Tone	
Main Idea	
Step 3	**S**ummary
지문 요약하기 (Paraphrasing)	
Step 4	**R**ecite
	요약문 말로 설명하기

50 Read the passage and follow the directions. [4 points]

> To understand why introverts and extroverts might react differently to the prospect of rewards, you have to know a little about brain structure. Our limbic system, which we share with the most primitive mammals and which Dorn calls the "old brain," is emotional and instinctive. It comprises various structures, including the amygdala, and it's highly interconnected with the nucleus accumbens, sometimes called the brain's "pleasure center." The old brain, according to Dorn, is constantly telling us, "Yes, yes, yes! Eat more, drink more, take lots of risk, go for all the gusto you can get, and above all, do not think!". The reward-seeking, pleasure-loving part of the old brain is what Dorn believes spurred people to treat their life savings like chips at the casino. We also have a "new brain" called the neocortex, which evolved many thousands of years after the limbic system. The new brain is responsible for thinking, planning, language, and decision-making—some of the very faculties that make us human. Although the new brain also plays a significant role in our emotional lives, it's the seat of rationality. Its job, according to Dorn, includes saying, "No, no, no! Don't do that, because it's dangerous, makes no sense, and is not in your best interests, or those of your family, or of society." The old brain and the new brain do work together, but not always efficiently. Sometimes they're actually in conflict, and then our decisions are a function of which one is sending out stronger signals.

In the given passage, identify the analogy used to exemplify impulsivity or sensational crisis the writer provides. Also, which of the two parts of the brain would be sending stronger signals in a speaker of three languages?

_____
_____
_____
_____

NOTE

Step 1	**S**urvey
Key Words	
Signal Words	
Step 2	**R**eading
Purpose	
Pattern of Organization	
Tone	
Main Idea	
Step 3	**S**ummary
지문 요약하기 (Paraphrasing)	
Step 4	**R**ecite

요약문 말로 설명하기

51 Read the passage and follow the directions. [4 points]

> Corot, the most prolific and influential landscape painter of the nineteenth century, had declined an invitation to join the Impressionist exhibition, but his influence was clearly felt in many of the works shown there by artists such as Monet, Pissarro, and Renoir. Corot, like many other artists, had sketched outdoors but used his sketches to create works in the studio. These works had the finish, particularly with regard to paint handling and compositional balance, that was an integral element of academic art. The Impressionists, however, not only made sketches but also painted finished works in the open, which transformed their style by preserving the spontaneity of direct observation. They adopted colors that more accurately reflected actual visual experience and avoided using blacks and browns for shadows and modeling. As a result, their paintings emphasized color, light, and atmospheric effects. Moreover, their relatively loose and open brushwork underscored their freedom from the meticulously detailed _____ manner that previously had been central to French painting.

Fill in the blank with the ONE most appropriate word from the passage. Second, explain the main difference between Corot and Impressionist's paintings, according to the passage.

NOTE

Step 1	**S**urvey
Key Words	
Signal Words	
Step 2	**R**eading
Purpose	
Pattern of Organization	
Tone	
Main Idea	
Step 3	**S**ummary
지문 요약하기 (Paraphrasing)	
Step 4	**R**ecite
	요약문 말로 설명하기

52 Read the passage and follow the directions. [4 points]

No one civilization can possibly utilize in its mores the whole potential range of human behavior. Every society, beginning with some inclination in one direction or another, carries its preference farther and farther, integrating itself more and more completely upon its chosen basis, and discarding those types of behaviors that are uncongenial. Most of those organizations of personality that seem to us more incontrovertibly abnormal have been used by different civilizations in the very foundations of their institutional life. Conversely, the most valued traits of our normal individuals have been looked on in differently organized cultures as aberrant. Normality, in short, within a very wide range, is culturally defined. The very eyes with which we see the problem are conditioned by the long traditional habits of our own society.

It is a point that has been made more often in relation to ethics than in relation to psychiatry. We do not any longer make the mistake of deriving the morality of our own locality and decade directly from the inevitable constitution of human nature. We do not elevate it to the dignity of a first principle. We recognize that _____ differs in every society, and is a convenient term for socially approved habits. Mankind has always preferred to say, "It is morally good" rather than "It is habitual." But historically the two phrases are synonymous.

Identify the ONE most appropriate word from the passage that most appropriately fills in the blank. Then, write how our society's normal behavior could be defined by differently-organized cultures.

NOTE

Step 1	**S**urvey
Key Words	
Signal Words	
Step 2	**R**eading
Purpose	
Pattern of Organization	
Tone	
Main Idea	
Step 3	**S**ummary
지문 요약하기 (Paraphrasing)	
Step 4	**R**ecite
	요약문 말로 설명하기

53 Read the passage and follow the directions. [4 points]

> Many Asian cultures are team-oriented, but not in the way that Westerners think of teams. Individuals in Asia see themselves as part of a greater whole—whether family, corporation, or community—and place tremendous value on harmony within their group. They often subordinate their own desires to the group's interests, accepting their place in its hierarchy. Western culture, by contrast, is organized around the _____. We see ourselves as self-contained units; our destiny is to express ourselves, to follow our bliss, to be free of undue restraint, to achieve the one thing that we, and we alone, were brought into this world to do. We may be gregarious, but we don't submit to group will, or at least we don't like to think we do. We love and respect our parents, but bridle at notions like filial piety, with their implications of subordination and restraint. When we get together with others, we do so as self-contained units having fun with, competing with, standing out from, jockeying for position with, and, yes, loving, other self-contained units. It makes sense, then, that Westerners value boldness and verbal skill, traits that promote individuality, while Asians prize quiet, humility, and sensitivity, which foster group cohesion. If you live in a collective, then things will go a lot more smoothly if you behave with restraint, even submission.

In the given passage, choose the ONE most appropriate word to fill the blank. You may change the word form if necessary. Second, explain how Asians act with family in contrast to Westerners.

_____
_____
_____
_____

NOTE

Step 1	Survey
Key Words	
Signal Words	
Step 2	**Reading**
Purpose	
Pattern of Organization	
Tone	
Main Idea	
Step 3	**Summary**
지문 요약하기 (Paraphrasing)	
Step 4	**Recite**
	요약문 말로 설명하기

54 Read the passage and follow the directions. [4 points]

> The ancient stone statues at San Agustín are among the most mysterious pre-Columbian archaeological artefacts. So far archaeologists have discovered 40 large burial mounds containing 600 likenesses of mythical animals, gods and chieftains in what is South America's largest complex of megalithic statues. Like other sites in the region, San Agustín has suffered plunder. Konrad Preuss, a German anthropologist who led the first European excavations there, shipped 35 statues that he found to a museum in Berlin, where they remain. This history has made the local inhabitants, who live from tourist visits to the site, suspicious. So it proved to be when by the national museum made a plan to take 20 of the statues to the capital, Bogotá, a ten-hour drive away, for a three-month exhibition to mark the centenary of Preuss's discovery of the site. Aware of the sensitivity of removing the statues even temporarily, anthropologists from the Colombian Institute of Anthropology held town meetings to explain the importance of allowing them to be seen by a wider public. But the locals said they worried that the objects would not return, or would be swapped for replicas. As the date for the exhibition neared, they began making demands, such as asking for a new drinking-water system for the town in exchange for letting the statues go. No deal was agreed. On the day last month when the sculptures were to travel to Bogotá, locals blockaded the road and prevented workers from loading the trucks. The museum has adopted its own form of protest. The exhibition opened, minus statues, on November 28. Light is projected where the statues would have been; guides use a virtual-reality program and tablet computers to show visitors a 3D image of what was meant to be there. The museum has taken a robust position: the opening display invites visitors to consider "the emptiness and silence that emerge when a few people claim exclusive right over our heritage, trampling the cultural liberties of all Colombians."

Describe the financial significance the statues hold for villagers. Then, explain what earlier incident might have created distrust amidst villagers as mentioned above. Do not copy more than FOUR consecutive words in your answer.

2S2R 유형

NOTE

Step 1	**S**urvey
Key Words	
Signal Words	
Step 2	**R**eading
Purpose	
Pattern of Organization	
Tone	
Main Idea	
Step 3	**S**ummary
지문 요약하기 (Paraphrasing)	
Step 4	**R**ecite
	요약문 말로 설명하기

A형 서술형

55 **Read the passage and follow the directions.** [4 points]

> The Englishmen who were quickly populating the Atlantic seaboard from the Carolinas to New England had no monopoly on the New World. French and Dutch explorers had also been busy, and both nations were carving out separate territories in North America. The Dutch founded New Netherlands in the Hudson Valley of present-day New York State, basing their claims upon the exploration of Henry Hudson in 1609.
>
> An Englishman, Hudson was hired by a Dutch company that wanted to find the Northeast Passage, the sea route to China along the northern rim of Asia. In 1609, Hudson set off instead, aboard the Half Moon, for the northwest alternative. Sailing down the Atlantic coast, he entered Chesapeake Bay before making a U-turn and heading back north to explore the Hudson River as far upriver as Albany. Noting the absence of tides, he correctly assumed that this route did not lead to the Pacific.
>
> England was flexing its new muscles in the early 1600s, but it was the Dutch who had become the true world power in maritime matters by building the world's largest merchant marine fleet. There was literally not a place in the known world of that day in which the Dutch did not have a hand in matters. Amsterdam had become the busiest and richest city in the European world. In 1621, the Dutch West India Company was formed with the aim of taking over trade between Europe and the New World, and the Dutch soon took from the Portuguese control of the lucrative slave and sugar trading outpost in 1624. Two years later, the trading village of New Amsterdam, later to be renamed New York, was established at the mouth of the Hudson. The Dutch West India Company did more than trade and set up colonies. In 1628, the Dutch Admiral Piet Hein captured a Spanish treasure fleet, pirating away enough silver to provide company shareholders with a 75-percent dividend.

Identify the major error in European navigation in the given passage. Second, identify the most powerful European force in the Americas in the seventeenth century.

NOTE

Step 1	**S**urvey
Key Words	
Signal Words	
Step 2	**R**eading
Purpose	
Pattern of Organization	
Tone	
Main Idea	
Step 3	**S**ummary
지문 요약하기 (Paraphrasing)	
Step 4	**R**ecite
	요약문 말로 설명하기

56 Read the passage and follow the directions. [4 points]

There are today about 190 million people in the world who live in a country other than the one in which they were born—nearly 60 percent of them are in rich countries (about 36 million in Europe and 38 million in the United States). People migrate primarily for economic reasons, but some do so to escape political and religious oppression. The 38 million foreign-born people who live in the United States represent 12.6 percent of the U.S. population. Of these, 11 million, or nearly 30 percent, entered the nation illegally. Most nations impose restrictions on immigration to reduce the inflow of low-skilled people (while often encouraging the immigration of highly skilled and technical people). Migration is generally more restricted and regulated than the international flow of goods, services and capital.

In general, _____ flows more freely across national boundaries than people. Financial or portfolio capital (bank loans and bonds) generally move to nations and markets where interest rates are higher, and foreign direct investments in plants and firms flow to nations where expected profits are higher. This leads to more efficient use of capital and generally benefits both lenders and borrowers. During the 1970s, Middle Eastern nations deposited a great deal of their huge earnings from petroleum exports in New York and London banks, which then lent (recycled) them to Latin American and Asian governments and corporations. During the 1980s, Japan invested a large chunk of its huge export earnings in financial assets and real estate and set up corporate subsidiaries in the United States. Since the mid-1980s, the United States has become an increasingly large net borrower from the rest of the world to cover its excess of spending over production. Global banks established branches in major international monetary centers around the world, nearly $3 trillion of foreign currencies are exchanged each day by around-the-clock trading in world financial centers, and newly-established sovereign funds (financial institutions owned by Middle Eastern petroleum exporting nations, Singapore, China, Russia, and Brazil) are making huge investments of all kinds all over the world. Financial markets are globalized as never before. The downside is that when a financial crisis starts in one country it quickly spreads to others.

Fill in the blank with the ONE most appropriate word from the passage. Second, state the reason that can be inferred that the United States has drawn a large immigrant population.

___

Step 1	Survey
Key Words	
Signal Words	
Step 2	**Reading**
Purpose	
Pattern of Organization	
Tone	
Main Idea	
Step 3	**Summary**
지문 요약하기 (Paraphrasing)	
Step 4	**Recite**
요약문 말로 설명하기	

57 Read the passage and follow the directions. [4 points]

> A very large number of people cease when quite young to add anything to a limited stock of judgments. After a certain age, say 25, they consider that their education finished. It is perhaps natural that having passed through that painful and boring process, expressly called education, they should suppose it over and think that they are equipped for life to label every event as it occurs and drop it into its given pigeonhole. But one who has a label ready for everything does not bother to observe any more, even such ordinary happenings as he had observed for himself, with attention, before he went to school. He merely acts and reacts. For people who have stopped noticing, the only possible new or renewed experience, and therefore new knowledge, is from a work of art. Because that is the only kind of experience which they are prepared to receive on its own terms, they will come out from their shells and expose themselves to music, to a play, to a book, because it is the accepted method of enjoying <u>such things</u>. True, even to plays and books they may bring artistic prejudices which prevent them from seeing that play or comprehending that book. Their artistic sensibilities may be as crusted over as their minds. But it is part of an artist's job to break crusts, or let us say rather that artists who work for the public and not merely for themselves are interested in breaking crusts because they want to communicate their intuitions.

Describe to what the underlined "such things" refer. Second, complete the following sentence by filling in the blank with the TWO most appropriate consecutive words from the passage.

> The writer sees the artist as a man charged with the responsibility for _____ of people's routinized thought patterns.

NOTE

Step 1	Survey
Key Words	
Signal Words	
Step 2	**Reading**
Purpose	
Pattern of Organization	
Tone	
Main Idea	
Step 3	**Summary**
지문 요약하기 (Paraphrasing)	
Step 4	**Recite**
	요약문 말로 설명하기

58 Read the passage and follow the directions. [4 points]

> An auction is usually advertised beforehand with full particulars of the articles to be sold and where and when they can be viewed by prospective buyers. If the advertisement cannot give full details, catalogues are printed, and each group of goods to be sold together, called a "lot", is usually given a number. The auctioneer need not begin with Lot 1 and continue in numerical order. He may wait until he registers the fact that certain dealers are in the room and then produce the lots they are likely to be interested in. The auctioneer's services are paid for in the form of a percentage of the price the goods are sold for. The auctioneer therefore has a direct interest in pushing up the bidding as high as possible. The auctioneer must know fairly accurately the current market values of the goods he is selling, and he should be acquainted with regular buyers of such goods. He will not waste time by starting the bidding too ____①____. He will also play on the rivalries among his buyers and succeed in getting a high price by encouraging two business competitors to bid against each other. It is largely on his advice that a seller will fix a "reserve" price, that is, a price below which the goods cannot be sold. Even the best auctioneers, however, find it difficult to stop a ② "knock-out" whereby dealers illegally arrange beforehand not to bid against each other, but nominate one of themselves as the only bidder, in the hope of buying goods at extremely low prices. If such a knock-out comes off, the real auction sale takes place privately afterwards among the dealers.

Fill in the blank with the ONE most appropriate word from the passage. Second, explain why a "knock-out" is arranged.

_____
_____
_____
_____

NOTE

Step 1	**S**urvey
Key Words	
Signal Words	
Step 2	**R**eading
Purpose	
Pattern of Organization	
Tone	
Main Idea	
Step 3	**S**ummary
지문 요약하기 (Paraphrasing)	
Step 4	**R**ecite
	요약문 말로 설명하기

59 Read the passage and follow the directions. [4 points]

> Traditional research has confronted only Mexican and United States interpretations of Mexican-American culture. Now we must also examine the culture as we Mexican-Americans have experienced it, passing from a sovereign people to compatriots with newly arriving settlers to, finally, a conquered people—<u>a charter minority on our own land</u>. When the Spanish first came to Mexico, they intermarried with and absorbed the culture of the indigenous Indians. This policy of colonization through acculturation was continued when Mexico acquired Texas in the early 1800s and brought the indigenous Indians into Mexican life and government. In the 1820s, United States citizens migrated to Texas, attracted by land suitable for cotton. As their numbers became more substantial, their policy of acquiring land by subduing native populations began to dominate. The two ideologies clashed repeatedly, culminating in a military conflict that led to victory for the United States. Thus, suddenly deprived of our parent culture, we had to evolve uniquely Mexican-American modes of thought and action in order to survive.

Explain why the author employs the phrase "a charter minority on our own land" in the first paragraph. Second, describe the writer's primary purpose in the passage.

NOTE

Step 1	Survey
Key Words	
Signal Words	
Step 2	**Reading**
Purpose	
Pattern of Organization	
Tone	
Main Idea	
Step 3	**Summary**
지문 요약하기 (Paraphrasing)	
Step 4	**Recite**
	요약문 말로 설명하기

B형 서술형

01 Read the passage and follow the directions. [4 points]

Throughout the last 400 years, during which the growth of science had gradually shown men how to acquire knowledge of the ways of nature and mastery over natural forces, the clergy have fought a losing battle against science, in astronomy and geology, in anatomy and physiology, in biology and psychology and sociology. Ousted from one position, they have taken up another. After being worsted in astronomy, they did their best to prevent the rise of geology; they fought against Darwin in biology, and at the present time they fight against scientific theories of psychology and education. At each stage, they try to make the public forget their earlier obscurantism, in order that their present obscurantism may not be recognized for what it is. Let us note a few instances of irrationality among the clergy since the rise of science, and then inquire whether the rest of mankind are any better.

When Benjamin Franklin invented the lightning rod, the clergy, both in England and America, with the enthusiastic support of George III, condemned it as an impious attempt to defeat the will of God. For, as all right-thinking people were aware, lightning is a form of punishment sent by God to address impiety or some other grave sins—the virtuous are never struck by lightning. Therefore if God wants to strike any one, Benjamin Franklin ought not to defeat His design; indeed, to do so is helping criminals to escape. But God was equal to the occasion, if we are to believe the eminent Dr. Price, one of the leading divines of Boston. Lightning having been rendered ineffectual by the "iron points invented by the sagacious Dr. Franklin," Massachusetts was shaken by earthquakes, which Dr. Price perceived to be due to God's wrath at the "iron points." In a sermon on the subject he said, "In Boston are more erected than elsewhere in New England, and Boston is more dreadfully shaken."

Apparently, however, Providence gave up all hope of curing Boston of its wickedness, for, though lightning rods became more and more common, earthquakes in Massachusetts have remained rare. Nevertheless, Dr. Price's point of view, or something very like it, is still held by one of the most influential of living men. When, at one time, there were several bad earthquakes in India, Mahatma Gandhi solemnly warned his compatriots that these disasters had been sent as a(n) _____ for their sins.

Fill in the blank with the ONE most appropriate word from the passage. Second, explain the intended meaning of the underlined part as interpreted by Dr. Price. Do Not copy more than FOUR consecutive words from the passage.

NOTE

Step 1	Survey
Key Words	
Signal Words	
Step 2	**Reading**
Purpose	
Pattern of Organization	
Tone	
Main Idea	
Step 3	**Summary**
지문 요약하기 (Paraphrasing)	
Step 4	**Recite**
	요약문 말로 설명하기

02 Read the passage and follow the directions. [4 points]

Progress has many dimensions. For primitive peoples and for most of the less developed countries of the world, it signifies a reduction in infant mortality, an increase in life spans, and an extension of _____. For the developed world, which may have achieved life spans close to the limit and in which infant mortality has fallen close to zero, while over 95 percent of the population can read and write, progress entails improvements different in kind and in degree. Simple literacy is no longer enough. Instead one looks for a rising level of education, a betterment of health for all ages and groups of the population, and for an extension in the command over resources. Increased knowledge frees people intellectually, while improved health makes for a better life.

Not all change is progress, especially to all people. Many men and women want to maintain the status quo; a goodly number want to halt what others might call progress. As I write these words, I am sitting on a balcony in a remote Greek mountain village. When I first came to this idyllic spot, the town was without electricity. Many, mainly visitors, opposed as an unaesthetic intrusion the stringing of power lines from house to house. To the natives, electricity, which made possible light and refrigeration, provided highly desirable progress. Without that innovation, this village would be dead today, for few would have continued coming here. The local population, which winters in the lowlands, would have remained in their cold-weather homes. During early visits there was no alternative to throwing our trash and garbage down a ravine about 100 feet from our cottage and right behind other houses. Now, with affluence, the city provides twice weekly trash pick-ups, has posted no littering signs at the local picnic spring, and has placed trash cans at strategic locations. Richer means cleaner!

When my wife first came to this village, she rode a donkey. Today the village has TVs, washing machines, tractors and telephones, but no donkeys. Twenty-five years ago, the only sounds were of chickens cackling, goats' bells, and donkeys braying; today these sounds are masked by the noise of motor cycles, car horns and chain saws. Is this progress? To those who live here, yes; to those of us who visit, it is a bit sad, although the beauty of the spot remains unaffected.

Overall, a rising per capita income does not necessarily constitute betterment for mankind. <u>Telephones that wake you from a pleasant afternoon's nap on a warm day in sunny Greece do not augment progress.</u>

Fill in the blank with the ONE most appropriate word from the passage. Second, explain what the writer of the passage mainly argues in the underlined part. Do Not copy more than FOUR consecutive words from the passage.

NOTE

Step 1	Survey
Key Words	
Signal Words	
Step 2	**Reading**
Purpose	
Pattern of Organization	
Tone	
Main Idea	
Step 3	**Summary**
지문 요약하기 (Paraphrasing)	
Step 4	**Recite**
	요약문 말로 설명하기

03 Read the passage and follow the directions. [4 points]

Organic solidarity refers to the social cohesion that arises from the interdependence of individuals within a society. Developed by French sociologist Émile Durkheim in his book *Division of Labour in Society* (1893), it posited that as societies become more complex and industrialized, the division of labor within them also increases, leading to a greater interdependence among individuals.

Durkheim argued that in traditional societies, mechanical solidarity prevails, where individuals share similar values, beliefs and customs, and there is little division of labor. In these societies, social cohesion is maintained by the similarity of individuals, and the collective consciousness is strong. However, as societies become more complex and industrialized, the division of labor increases, leading to a greater differentiation of roles and functions within society. As a result, individuals become more specialized and interdependent, and social cohesion is maintained by the interdependence of individuals, rather than by their _____. Durkheim believed that organic solidarity is a natural and necessary aspect of social evolution. As societies become more complex, the division of labor becomes more specialized, and individuals become more interdependent. This interdependence leads to a greater division of labor, which in turn leads to greater social cohesion.

Organic solidarity is important because it allows for the efficient functioning of society. As individuals specialize in different roles and tasks, they become more efficient and productive, and society as a whole benefits. Additionally, organic solidarity leads to a greater sense of social cohesion and integration, as individuals come to rely on one another for the satisfaction of their needs and wants.

Critics of Durkheim's theory argue that organic solidarity may lead to a loss of community and social cohesion. As individuals become more specialized and interdependent, they may become more isolated and disconnected from one another. Additionally, as society becomes more complex, the division of labor may lead to social inequality and stratification. However, Durkheim's theory can be seen as an ideal type and not all societies will reach this level of organic solidarity. Furthermore, contemporary sociologists argue that organic solidarity can be strengthened by ensuring that it is inclusive, and by addressing issues of social inequality and stratification.

Fill in the blank with the ONE most appropriate word from the passage. Second, describe the criticism of organic solidarity, in terms of social cohesion. Do Not copy more than FOUR consecutive words from the passage.

___
___
___
___
___

NOTE

Step 1	Survey
Key Words	
Signal Words	
Step 2	**Reading**
Purpose	
Pattern of Organization	
Tone	
Main Idea	
Step 3	**Summary**
지문 요약하기 (Paraphrasing)	
Step 4	**Recite**
	요약문 말로 설명하기

04 Read the passage and follow the directions. [4 points]

The history of standardized entrance exams can be traced back to ancient civilizations but became more formally recognized and widely adopted with the development of educational systems in the modern era. These exams have played a significant role in shaping educational access and assessment across the globe. Standardized entrance exams exist primarily for two main reasons.

Standardized exams exist because they provide a consistent measure to evaluate the knowledge, skills, and critical thinking abilities of applicants. By testing on a common set of criteria, educational institutions can determine whether students have the foundational understanding and intellectual capacity required for success in their programs. These exams often cover a broad range of subjects or specific areas relevant to the field of study, helping to identify students who are prepared for the rigors of higher education or specialized programs.

Standardized testing also can create a level playing field where students from diverse educational backgrounds, schools, and regions can be assessed using the same criteria. This helps to mitigate biases and inconsistencies that can arise from subjective evaluations or varying standards across different schools. By providing a uniform benchmark, standardized exams strive to ensure that admissions decisions are based on quantifiable, comparable data, thus promoting fairness in the selection process.

These reasons underscore the role of standardized exams in the admissions landscape. However, it cannot be overlooked that standardized tests tend to perpetuate socioeconomic disparities and focus too heavily on rote memorization and specific types of intelligence, such as mathematical and verbal skills, at the expense of creativity, critical thinking, and other forms of intelligence not easily measured by standardized tests.

Write a summary following the guidelines below.

Guidelines
• Summarize the above passage in ONE paragraph. • Provide a topic sentence, two supporting ideas, and a concluding sentence based on the passage. • Do NOT copy more than FOUR consecutive words from the passage.

NOTE

Step 1	**S**urvey
Key Words	
Signal Words	
Step 2	**R**eading
Purpose	
Pattern of Organization	
Tone	
Main Idea	
Step 3	**S**ummary
지문 요약하기 (Paraphrasing)	
Step 4	**R**ecite
	요약문 말로 설명하기

05 Read the passage and follow the directions. [4 points]

> Yglesias argues that "nostalgia is a dead end," and in some ways he is right. He's right that the psychic power of conservative nostalgic appeals trades on the audience's vague sense of the Good Old Days, while offering no positive policy solutions to achieve something like a better future. He is also right that nostalgia is largely subjective—we are often nostalgic for just those times when we were younger, had more disposable income, were less burdened with responsibilities, or were healthier than we are today. Fair enough.
>
> To demonstrate his point, he explains how much richer and better off we are now. We have more cars, we have more microwaves, bigger homes, etc. Yet if today is so great, why do so many people—from very opposite political worlds, and from very different age cohorts—find the mid-century so attractive?
>
> In 2016 the *New York Times* published the results of a Morning Consult survey that asked "When Was America Greatest?" The results confirm a particular fondness for the mid-century. Republicans tended to laud the 1950s (and Ronnie Reagan's 1980s) as the halcyon days. Curiously, however, among Democrats, the *Times* notes that "Mr. Sanders's voters were more likely to pick a year from the 1960s, and more of the Clinton supporters chose best years in the 1990s, when her husband was president."
>
> For those who did live through the period the affection seems even more profound. In his book *Stayin' Alive*, Jefferson Cowie notes, the decade really was a revelation for the working-class, with workers' wages increasing by almost 62 percent between 1947 and 1972. By comparison, between 1998 and 2022, real median household wages only increased by 13.88 percent. As much talk as there is about the impressive growth of the Clinton years, the 1990s was nothing like "liberation."

Economic equality, political comity, social fraternity, and cultural solidarity culminate in the mid-century, the late 1950s and 1960s. Since then, the social world in the US has been slouching toward dissolution.

In terms of income and wealth, our society hit peak equality in the late 1960s. And this is not only true in terms of the gap between the very top and the very bottom. Inequality decreased even within the middle and lower classes during the period between 1913 and around 1970. Additionally, black Americans experienced the fastest wage growth and the smallest black-white wage gap during the late 1950s and early '60s. The increasing economic equality of this time was what made the Voting Rights Act and the Civil Rights Act conceivable political programs. And it is a tragedy of history that the trend to greater equality stalled and reversed after the successful passage of these acts.

A dive into mid-century American history uncovers how a strong labor movement was pivotal in building social unity, equality, and advancing civil rights. While _____ might seem like a blind alley, the past holds valuable lessons for shaping a better future.

Fill in the blank with the ONE most appropriate word from the passage. Second, explain the main reason the writer mentions "the Clinton years" in the passage. Do Not copy more than FOUR consecutive words from the passage.

NOTE

Step 1	**S**urvey
Key Words	
Signal Words	
Step 2	**R**eading
Purpose	
Pattern of Organization	
Tone	
Main Idea	
Step 3	**S**ummary
지문 요약하기 (Paraphrasing)	
Step 4	**R**ecite
	요약문 말로 설명하기

06 Read the passage and follow the directions. [4 points]

It is best approached indirectly, through the parable of the blind scholars and their elephant: Each touches, senses, and knows a part of the elephant and declares the elephant to be like what they touch: tusklike, trunklike, or taillike. Each hears the other saying something incompatible with the thing that they themselves touch.

The first limit to the parable is that maybe there's no whole elephant to be seen, either. A scholar who could see the elephant would not know any better than the blind ones, because while the account by the scholar who sees might include the grey color of its skin, they may know nothing of its texture or smell. Nobody gets to know the totality.

The second limit to this parable is that it may not even be possible to combine all of these partial accounts of the elephant into a true and whole picture of the elephant as a totality, as a world. The parts don't quite add up to a whole. Each way of knowing shapes in part the thing it comes to know, producing parts that are parts of different wholes. Knowing is never quite going to come together again, and there may be nothing at all helpful any more in the fiction that it might.

This was always the <u>paradox</u> about the project of knowing the world. The knowing depended on myths that posit a whole, unknown world at the start and another, different whole world, the unity of the world of knowledge, at the end. The knowing is in between two things that are some kind of non-knowledge, an imagined start and a projected future. Nobody much believes in this anymore. Knowledge has lost its religion, that which bound it together, through time and across the disciplines. It is futile to try and hide this from anyone, least of all ourselves. The university, like the church before it, is now a habit without gods. Knowledge doesn't add up. Nothing guarantees that its parts are parts of a(n) _____.

Fill in the blank with the ONE most appropriate word from the passage. Second, explain what the underlined "paradox" highlights in the context of the passage. Do Not copy more than FOUR consecutive words from the passage.

NOTE

Step 1	Survey
Key Words	
Signal Words	
Step 2	**Reading**
Purpose	
Pattern of Organization	
Tone	
Main Idea	
Step 3	**Summary**
지문 요약하기 (Paraphrasing)	
Step 4	**Recite**
	요약문 말로 설명하기

07 Read the passage and follow the directions. [4 points]

Recent research has shown that engravings in a cave in La Roche-Cotard (France), which has been sealed for thousands of years, were actually made by Neanderthals. The findings reveal that the Neanderthals were in fact the first humans with an appreciation of _____.

When the French archaeologist Jean-Claude Marquet entered the La Roche-Cotard cave in the Loire Valley for the first time back in 1974, he suspected that the fine lines on the wall could be of human origin. He also found scrapers and other retouched pieces known as Mousterian stone artifacts that suggested the cave had been used by Neanderthals.

Were the marks on the wall evidence of early Neanderthal artistic activity? Posing this question raised the possibility of breaking with the consensus of the time, which largely assumed that *Homo neanderthalensis* lacked any higher cognitive abilities. Fearing he would be unable to provide sufficient scientific evidence to prove his hypothesis, Marquet left the cave untouched for almost 40 years.

Together with an international team, he made another attempt in 2016. This time he was accompanied by Dr. Dorota Wojtczak from Integrative Prehistoric and Archaeological Science (IPAS) at the Department of Environmental Sciences of the University of Basel, who specializes in archaeological use-wear analysis. Their task was to use modern methods to prove the human origin of these wall engravings. The researchers recently published their findings in the journal *PLoS ONE*.

First with photos and drawings and later with a 3D scanner, the marks in the tuff rock of the cave wall were meticulously recorded. In her laboratory in Basel, Wojtczak compared these samples from the cave with tuff she had worked on experimentally with wood, bone and stone tools, as well as with her hands. The research clearly showed that the cave marks were not made with tools, but by scratching with human fingers.

At the same time, the cave must have been sealed off by mud residues from the Loire and soil sediments for over 50,000 years before being rediscovered. This makes the La Roche-Cotard cave system a very special location—a veritable "time capsule." "At this time, 50,000 years ago, there were no modern humans in Europe, only Neanderthals," says Wojtczak. The wall marks and artifacts can therefore only come from these early humans.

While the clear geometric shapes with parallel and triangular lines suggest that these marks were not scribbled on the wall by chance, the researcher does not know what they represent. "But they could only have been made by someone who proceeded with planning and understanding," she says. And whether it was "art" as such, or a form of recording-keeping, is a matter of interpretation. Wojtczak is convinced that every investigation will help to further dismantle the traditional consensus of Neanderthals as mentally inferior humans, who lacked artistic activity.

Fill in the blank with the ONE most appropriate word from the passage. Second, explain why the La Roche-Cotard cave system is a special location according to the passage. Do NOT copy more than FOUR consecutive words from the passage.

NOTE

Step 1	Survey
Key Words	
Signal Words	
Step 2	**Reading**
Purpose	
Pattern of Organization	
Tone	
Main Idea	
Step 3	**Summary**
지문 요약하기 (Paraphrasing)	
Step 4	**Recite**
	요약문 말로 설명하기

08 Read the passage and follow the directions. [4 points]

> An online echo chamber is a type of virtual space where a particular perspective or ideology is reinforced and amplified, while alternative viewpoints are suppressed or marginalized. Online echo chambers can be found on a wide range of platforms, including social media, forums, and news websites, and they can have a significant impact on the way that people perceive and understand the world around them. The existence of online echo chambers has several negative consequences for both individuals and society as a whole.
>
> When individuals participate in echo chambers, they are primarily exposed to information and opinions that reinforce their pre-existing views, while alternative viewpoints are minimized or ignored. This can result in a skewed perception of reality, as the lack of exposure to diverse perspectives leads to a more polarized view on issues. Also, constant exposure to reinforcing opinions can diminish individuals' ability to critically assess information. This reduction in critical thinking skills can make individuals more susceptible to manipulation and less likely to engage in independent thought.
>
> Echo chambers can contribute to the fragmentation of society into insular groups that lack understanding and tolerance of each other. This fragmentation can weaken social cohesion and make it more challenging to address collective problems. Also, the democratic process relies on informed citizens engaging in healthy debate. Echo chambers can undermine this by creating fragmented realities where shared facts and common ground are elusive, making constructive public discourse difficult.
>
> To combat the negative consequences of online echo chambers, it is important for people to be aware of their existence and to make an effort to expose themselves to a diverse range of perspectives. This can involve following a variety of sources of information, engaging with people who have different viewpoints, and being open to considering alternative perspectives.

Write a summary following the guidelines below.

Guidelines
• Summarize the above passage in ONE paragraph. • Provide a topic sentence, two supporting ideas, and a concluding sentence based on the passage. • Do NOT copy more than FOUR consecutive words from the passage.

NOTE

Step 1	**S**urvey
Key Words	
Signal Words	
Step 2	**R**eading
Purpose	
Pattern of Organization	
Tone	
Main Idea	
Step 3	**S**ummary
지문 요약하기 (Paraphrasing)	
Step 4	**R**ecite
	요약문 말로 설명하기

09 Read the passage and follow the directions. [4 points]

Empathy can help people build strong friendships and close family ties. A new study reinforces the power of teaching and practicing empathy, especially during adolescence. New results from a long-term study published in the journal *Child Development* found that teens who received "empathic care" from their mother (the only parent included in the study) were able to pay it forward and show empathy to their close friends. The research further suggests that parental empathy is passed down from generation to generation: teenagers who developed empathy skills were more likely to have healthy adult relationships and a supportive parenting style with their own children more than a decade later. "This study is among the first to show that teenage friendships may play a role in predicting how we parent," says Jessica Stern, a postdoctoral fellow at the University of Virginia and first author of the study.

Longitudinal studies that link together different relationships across time are unique and impressive, says Lana Karasik, a psychology professor at the College of Staten Island, who was not involved in the study. "I have not seen anything like it," she says. "Usually, giant studies such as this one typically rely on self-reported behaviors. The incorporation of behavioral measures of the parent-to-adolescent and the adolescent-to-adolescent interactions was a big strength."

Previous research suggests that teenage years are an important period for building empathy along with other social and emotional skills. Teens also start to depend less on their parents, discover their own identities, become interested in understanding the perspectives of others and learn how to navigate social situations independently.

The new study is part of an ongoing project called KLIFF/VIDA (Kids, Lives, Families, Friends/Virginia Institute for Development in Adulthood). Since 1998 KLIFF/VIDA has followed 184 people from age 13 into their late 30s using surveys and in-person observations. The demographically diverse participants were recruited during middle school in the Charlottesville, Va., area. This project focused on the empathic care of mothers, but the researchers hope to include the effects of empathetic fathers in future follow-up studies.

In the Child Development study, the team invited teenagers, along with each participant's mother and one of their close friends, into the lab once a year and recorded six-minute conversations about a problem that the teen was having. The researchers looked for four main indicators of empathy: emotional engagement, support, solutions and understanding. Mothers who were emotionally engaged actively listened and asked thoughtful follow-up questions. Supportive parents often validated what their kid was feeling or offered comfort by expressing concern or sympathy. They also steered the conversation toward solutions while acknowledging their teen's needs. Their level of _____ regarding their teen's experiences was evaluated through the relevance of their suggestions and responses.

Fill in the blank with the ONE most appropriate word from the passage. Second, in what THREE methodological aspects is this new study valuable compared to previous ones? Do NOT copy more than FOUR consecutive words from the passage.

NOTE

Step 1	**S**urvey
Key Words	
Signal Words	
Step 2	**R**eading
Purpose	
Pattern of Organization	
Tone	
Main Idea	
Step 3	**S**ummary
지문 요약하기 (Paraphrasing)	
Step 4	**R**ecite
	요약문 말로 설명하기

10 Read the passage and follow the directions. [4 points]

Diderot was 52 years old and his daughter was about to be married, but he could not afford to provide a dowry. Despite his lack of wealth, Diderot's name was well-known because he was the co-founder and writer of *Encyclopédie*, one of the most comprehensive encyclopedias of the time.

When Catherine the Great, the Empress of Russia, heard of Diderot's financial troubles she offered to buy his library from him for £1000 GBP, which is approximately $50,000 USD in 2015 dollars. Suddenly, Diderot had money to spare. Shortly after this lucky sale, Diderot acquired a new scarlet robe. That's when everything went _____.

Diderot's scarlet robe was beautiful. So beautiful, in fact, that he immediately noticed how out of place it seemed when surrounded by the rest of his common possessions. In his words, there was "no more coordination, no more unity, no more beauty" between his robe and the rest of his items. The philosopher soon felt the urge to buy some new things to match the beauty of his robe.

He replaced his old rug with a new one from Damascus. He decorated his home with beautiful sculptures and a better kitchen table. He bought a new mirror to place above the mantle and his straw chair was relegated to the antechamber by a leather chair. These reactive purchases have become known as the Diderot Effect.

Like many others, I have fallen victim to the Diderot Effect. I recently bought a new car and I ended up purchasing all sorts of additional things to go inside it. I bought a tire pressure gauge, a car charger for my cell phone, an extra umbrella, a first aid kit, a pocket knife, a flashlight, emergency blankets, and even a seatbelt cutting tool.

Allow me to point out that I owned my previous car for nearly 10 years and at no point did I feel that any of the previously mentioned items were worth purchasing. And yet, after getting my shiny new car, I found myself falling into the same consumption spiral as Diderot.

The Diderot Effect tells us that your life is only going to have more things fighting to get in it, so you need to understand how to curate, eliminate, and focus on the things that matter to avoid going wrong.

Fill in the blank with the ONE most appropriate word from the passage. Second, explain what "The Diderot Effect" is. Do NOT copy more than FOUR consecutive words from the passage.

NOTE

Step 1	Survey
Key Words	
Signal Words	
Step 2	**Reading**
Purpose	
Pattern of Organization	
Tone	
Main Idea	
Step 3	**Summary**
지문 요약하기 (Paraphrasing)	
Step 4	**Recite**
	요약문 말로 설명하기

11 Read the passage and follow the directions. [4 points]

> The tug of war between employers and employees over the issue of returning to the office continues. Many companies are taking a firm stance on requiring their staff to resume work from the office. 38% of companies require full-time in-office work. There are a few reasons for this insistence.
>
> Employers are increasingly vocal about their concerns regarding employee engagement and the need for human connection. They argue that the synergy of in-person interactions and the spontaneous conversations that occur in a shared physical space are critical to fostering innovation, collaboration, and a shared corporate identity. For many organizations, these elements are seen as central to their success and difficult to maintain in a virtual environment.
>
> Companies are also worried about the potential for a dilution of their corporate culture if remote work continues indefinitely. The shared experiences that build camaraderie and a sense of belonging among employees are not easily replicated online, and many business leaders fear that without a return to the office, their company's unique culture could erode. In a 2022 Korn Ferry survey, two-thirds of 15,000 global executives agreed that corporate culture constitutes more than 30% of their company's market value. Many leaders believe that building and maintaining a strong culture requires everyone to occupy the same workplace at least some of the time.
>
> However, on the other side of the rope, employees are pulling for the continuation of remote work arrangements. Many employees prefer the flexibility and autonomy that comes with remote work. Therefore, it is necessary for both parties to find a middle ground that respects the needs and preferences of employees while addressing the concerns of employers. This compromise could include hybrid work models, which allow for a balance of remote and in-office work, fostering both flexibility and team cohesion.

Write a summary following the guidelines below.

--- Guidelines ---
- Summarize the above passage in ONE paragraph.
- Provide a topic sentence, two supporting ideas, and a concluding sentence based on the passage.
- Do NOT copy more than FOUR consecutive words from the passage.

NOTE

Step 1	Survey
Key Words	
Signal Words	
Step 2	**Reading**
Purpose	
Pattern of Organization	
Tone	
Main Idea	
Step 3	**Summary**
지문 요약하기 (Paraphrasing)	
Step 4	**Recite**
	요약문 말로 설명하기

12 Read the passage and follow the directions. [4 points]

I once tried to watch Andy Warhol's *Empire* (1964) for as long as I could. I lasted maybe twenty minutes. The whole eight-hour film is a single shot of the Empire State Building. It got boring, but then a bird flew by and it was like being struck by lightning. One could think of the subject of all Warhol's art as the act of paying attention. It is worth having Warhol in mind while reading Yves Citton's *The Ecology of Attention*. Warhol is not mentioned in it, but he does cover both ends of the attention problem. On the one hand, Warhol made work that is very demanding of attention; on the other, he got his own image to circulate as an instant attention attractor. He understood the value of attention.

He was not the first, of course. Citton begins with Gabriel Tarde, who starts a line of thinking about an economy of visibility whose currency is fame. It became an economy in a double sense, in that fame can be measured, and the attention it garners can be scarce. An increasing wealth of information means a scarcity of something else. Economists treat attention as a commodity, to be hoarded or strategically acquired. Citton wants to put some critical pressure on that view, by paying attention to what it leaves out. Perhaps the design of the attention-gathering apparatus is suboptimal.

Attention is not a new concern. The ancient art of rhetoric was about taking and holding it. Among the moderns, attention to innovation in style has long been a way of renewing attention. One might connect this to the way Sianne Ngai thinks about the aesthetics of the zany, interesting, and cute, each of which draws attention to, and also away from, aspects of modern life, to production, circulation, and the commodity, respectively. Warhol pioneered <u>forms of all three</u> as ways of attracting attention.

Citton offers an attention ecology rather than an attention economy. The latter tends to start with individualized attention as if it always existed, whereas an attention ecology takes an interest also in how attention regimes produce individuals in the first place. The key difference is that while a(n) _____ focuses on how attention is used or exchanged by individuals, an attention ecology is interested in the broader context—how attention itself is structured, influenced, and shaped by external factors, and how these processes contribute to the formation of individuals and their attention patterns. This ecology can be rather noisy, more like the turbulent information soup than the simple sender→receiver of the classic communication diagrams.

Fill in the blank with the TWO most appropriate consecutive words from the passage. Second, identify to what the underlined "forms of all three" refers. Do NOT copy more than FOUR consecutive words from the passage.

NOTE

Step 1	**S**urvey
Key Words	
Signal Words	
Step 2	**R**eading
Purpose	
Pattern of Organization	
Tone	
Main Idea	
Step 3	**S**ummary
지문 요약하기 (Paraphrasing)	
Step 4	**R**ecite
	요약문 말로 설명하기

13 Read the passage and follow the directions. [4 points]

What does _____ have to do with creativity? The answer could be "a lot." Individualism has long been thought to have a creative edge. Individualists resist social convention, the logic goes, and that pushback supports innovation. For instance, around the world individualistic cultures have more invention patents than collectivistic cultures do. That advantage remains even when we compare only countries with similar wealth. But a recent study suggests that people in collectivistic cultures actually do better with a particular type of creative thinking, which could be linked to what their ancestors farmed.

The new work comes from comparing communities in different parts of China. Although China scores high, as a nation, on measures of cultural collectivism, its 1.4 billion people are more than just a single culture. As my own work has explored, there are distinct individualistic and collectivistic communities within China. For example, people from areas north of the Yangtze River tend to be more individualistic, whereas people along the river and farther south are often more interdependent.

In the new study, published in *Frontiers in Psychology*, researchers investigated innovation with these two groups in mind. Although creativity is notoriously hard to measure, they used a drawing test created by psychologists. The team gave kids a sheet of paper with just a few basic elements printed on it: some dots here, squiggles there and a rectangle that suggested a drawing frame. The children got 15 minutes to draw what they wanted.

The kids could get "adaptive creativity" points for doodling in ways that connected the squiggles and lines into an original but unified image. Those that included an outside-the-box detail could get points for "boundary-breaking creativity." Researchers in China gave the test to 683 middle school students from north and south of the Yangtze River. There were no differences in the children's overall creativity. In other words, youngsters from individualistic communities did not have an edge in this task. In fact, when broken down into components, students from collectivistic regions scored higher in adaptive creativity. The middle schoolers from individualistic areas scored higher in boundary-breaking creativity.

Research with adults suggests that boundary-breaking creativity supports innovations that revolutionize a field. In line with that idea, the kids who scored high in boundary-breaking lived in parts of northern, more individualistic China, which has more patents for inventions. In contrast, adaptive creativity comes into play when people improve existing technologies and approaches, developing next-generation solutions that build on what has been done to date. This difference might explain why much of China's manufacturing sector, which has grown through incremental improvements, has sprung up in the southern, collectivist areas.

Fill in the blank with the ONE most appropriate word from the passage. Second, how do individualistic and collectivistic cultures within China influence different types of creative thinking in middle school students, according to the study published in *Frontiers in Psychology*? Do NOT copy more than FOUR consecutive words from the passage.

NOTE

Step 1	**S**urvey
Key Words	
Signal Words	
Step 2	**R**eading
Purpose	
Pattern of Organization	
Tone	
Main Idea	
Step 3	**S**ummary
지문 요약하기 (Paraphrasing)	
Step 4	**R**ecite
요약문 말로 설명하기	

14 Read the passage and follow the directions. [4 points]

On the first day of class, Jerry Uelsmann, a professor at the University of Florida, divided his film photography students into two groups. Everyone on the left side of the classroom, he explained, would be in the "quantity" group. They would be graded solely on the amount of work they produced. On the final day of class, he would tally the number of photos submitted by each student. One hundred photos would rate an A, ninety photos a B, eighty photos a C, and so on. Meanwhile, everyone on the right side of the room would be in the "quality" group. They would be graded only on the excellence of their work. They only needed to produce one photo during the semester, but to earn an A, it had to achieve perfection.

At the end of the term, he was surprised to find that all the best photos were produced by the quantity group. During the semester, these students were busy taking photos, experimenting with composition and lighting, testing out various methods in the darkroom, and learning from their mistakes. In the process of creating hundreds of photos, they honed their skills. Meanwhile, the quality group sat around speculating about _____. In the end, they had little to show for their efforts other than unverified theories and one mediocre photo.

It is easy to get bogged down trying to find the optimal plan for change: the fastest way to lose weight, the best program to build muscle, the perfect idea for a side hustle. We are so focused on figuring out the best approach that we never get around to taking action. As Voltaire once wrote, "The best is the enemy of the good."

It's not just art studios where repetitions matter. Whenever you put in consistent work and learn from your mistakes, incredible progress is the result. This is why I force myself to write a new article every Monday and Thursday. I can't predict which articles will be useful, but I know that <u>if I write two per week, then sometimes I'll hit the bullseye.</u>

2S2R 유형

Fill in the blank with the ONE most appropriate word from the passage. Second, explain what the writer of the passage argues in the underlined "if I write two per week, then sometimes I'll hit the bullseye." Do NOT copy more than FOUR consecutive words from the passage.

_____

_____

NOTE

Step 1	**S**urvey
Key Words	
Signal Words	
Step 2	**R**eading
Purpose	
Pattern of Organization	
Tone	
Main Idea	
Step 3	**S**ummary
지문 요약하기 (Paraphrasing)	
Step 4	**R**ecite
	요약문 말로 설명하기

15. Read the passage and follow the directions. [4 points]

Young people enjoy intrinsic pursuits naturally. As Picasso said, we are all born artists. The problem is, we grow up. "Kids are little spontaneity machines," says Edward Slingerland, a philosophy professor at the University of British Columbia. He recalls his daughter at an age when she couldn't walk a line from points A to B without zig-zagging jumps and somersaults. Few adults seek a return to this behavior. Why are kids little spontaneity machines?

One factor is dopamine, a brain chemical linked to motivation and reward, inspires spontaneous movements in both humans and mice, as discovered by Sandeep Robert Datta, a Harvard neurobiologist. Monitoring mouse brains in unfamiliar settings, Datta found that younger mice exhibit more random behavior, a pattern that peaks just before maturity when such spontaneity declines. In humans, exploring environments like cities can enhance understanding and resourcefulness. However, similar to mice, human dopamine levels decrease by about 10% each decade, reducing spontaneous activity as we age.

Another explanation for youthful spontaneity is neuroplasticity. The period of juvenile exuberance coincides with the brain being massively flexible and engaged in ongoing learning. Like dopamine, neuroplasticity declines after a certain point in life. With the juvenile-to-adult transition, neural circuits get locked to some extent into adult configurations. Spontaneity can be viewed as a measure of biological aging. These changes affect more than movement. Spontaneous thoughts also seem to peak when we're younger. College students and young adults engage in mind wandering up to 50% of the day. In older age, it typically declines to about 30%.

Young people exhibit a high degree of spontaneity driven by biological factors such as high dopamine levels and increased neuroplasticity. As individuals age, a decline in these biological elements corresponds with a reduced tendency for spontaneous thought and movement, illustrating a transition into more settled and predictable behaviors. However, engaging in regular creative and physical activities can help maintain higher levels of dopamine and neuroplasticity, potentially preserving spontaneity and adaptability well into adulthood.

Write a summary following the guidelines below.

---- Guidelines ----

- Summarize the above passage in ONE paragraph.
- Provide a topic sentence, two supporting ideas, and a concluding sentence based on the passage.
- Do NOT copy more than FOUR consecutive words from the passage.

NOTE

Step 1	**S**urvey
Key Words	
Signal Words	
Step 2	**R**eading
Purpose	
Pattern of Organization	
Tone	
Main Idea	
Step 3	**S**ummary
지문 요약하기 (Paraphrasing)	
Step 4	**R**ecite
	요약문 말로 설명하기

16 Read the passage and follow the directions. [4 points]

We don't choose our siblings the way we choose our partners and friends. Of course, we don't choose our parents either, but they usually make that up to us by sustaining us on the way to adulthood. Brothers and sisters are just sort of there. And yet, when it comes to our development, they can be more influential than parents. This holds whether they are older and cool, or younger and frustrating; whether we follow in their footsteps, or run screaming in the other direction.

Part of siblings' sway has to do with their sheer presence. Eighty-two percent of kids live with a sibling (a greater share than live with a father), and about 75 percent of 70-year-olds have a living sibling. For those of us who have brothers or sisters, our relationships with them will likely be the longest of our life.

Whether these relationships make our life better or worse is a more complicated question. On the upside, positive interactions with siblings during adolescence foster empathy, prosocial behavior, and academic achievement. This effect can be complicated by a full house, however. Kids with more siblings (a larger "sibship," to use the industry term) do worse in school—although the universality of this finding has been challenged by studies of Mormons and the entire population of Norway.

When a sibling relationship is bad, however, it can be really bad—as in messing-up-your-life bad. Tense sibling relationships make people more likely to use substances and to be depressed and anxious in adolescence. Moreover, sibling bullying makes a kid more likely to engage in self-harm as a teen and to become psychotic by age 18.

Whether a person models herself after her siblings or tries to distinguish herself has particularly important consequences. One study found that siblings who felt positively about each other tended to achieve similar education levels, while those who spent unequal time with their dad and perceived unequal parental treatment had diverging educational fortunes. Not that divergence is necessarily bad: Research suggests that as siblings' relationships with their parents grow more different over time, their relationship with each other may become warmer. And emulating your sibling can be a mistake, depending on what she's up to: Girls are more likely to get pregnant in their teens and teenagers are more likely to engage in risky behavior if an older sibling did so first.

One way or another, sibling influence is lasting. A study of more than 1 million Swedes found that one's risk of dying of a heart attack spikes after a sibling dies of one, due not only to shared DNA but also to the stress of losing such a key figure. Which makes sense: Most of us are different people than we'd have been if our brothers or sisters were never born. <u>Siblings seem like they're just there only until they aren't.</u>

Explain the reason the writer of the passage mentions Mormons. Second, what does the underlined "Siblings seem like they're just there only until they aren't" mean? Do NOT copy more than FOUR consecutive words from the passage.

NOTE

Step 1	**S**urvey
Key Words	
Signal Words	
Step 2	**R**eading
Purpose	
Pattern of Organization	
Tone	
Main Idea	
Step 3	**S**ummary
지문 요약하기 (Paraphrasing)	
Step 4	**R**ecite
	요약문 말로 설명하기

17 Read the passage and follow the directions. [4 points]

Gender influences our friendships and has received much attention, as people try to figure out how different men and women's friendships are. There is a conception that men's friendships are less intimate than women's based on the stereotype that men do not express emotions. In fact, men report a similar amount of intimacy in their friendships as women but are less likely than women to explicitly express affection verbally (e.g., saying "I love you") and nonverbally (e.g., through touching or embracing) toward their same-gender friends, though they still engage in positive expressions of closeness through shared activities and support.

This is not surprising, given the societal taboos against same-gender expressions of affection, especially between men, even though an increasing number of men are more comfortable expressing affection toward other men and women. However, researchers have wondered if men communicate affection in more implicit ways that are still understood by the other friend. Men may use shared activities as a way to express closeness—for example, by doing favors for each other, engaging in friendly competition, joking, sharing resources, or teaching each other new skills. Some scholars have argued that there is a bias toward viewing intimacy as feminine, which may have skewed research on men's friendships. While verbal expressions of intimacy through self-disclosure have been noted as important features of women's friendships, activity sharing has been the focus in men's friendships. I don't argue that one gender's friendships are better than the other's. And the differences regarding expressions of intimacy are not large enough to impact the actual practice of friendships.

Cross-gender friendships diminish in late childhood and early adolescence as boys and girls segregate into separate groups for many activities and socializing, reemerge as possibilities in late adolescence, and reach a peak potential in the college years of early adulthood. Later, adults with spouses or partners are less likely to have cross-sex friendships than single people, which may reflect the evolving priorities and commitments that often accompany long-term relationships.

In any case, research studies have identified several _____ outcomes of cross-gender friendships. Men and women report that they get a richer understanding of how the other gender thinks and feels. It seems these friendships fulfill interaction needs not as commonly met in same-gender friendships. For example, men reported more than women that they rely on their cross-gender friendships for emotional support. Similarly, women reported that they enjoyed the activity-oriented friendships they had with men.

Fill in the blank with the ONE most appropriate word from the passage. Second, based on the passage, why might the dynamics of long-term relationships influence the nature or prevalence of cross-gender friendships in adulthood? Do NOT copy more than FOUR consecutive words from the passage.

NOTE

Step 1	**S**urvey
Key Words	
Signal Words	
Step 2	**R**eading
Purpose	
Pattern of Organization	
Tone	
Main Idea	
Step 3	**S**ummary
지문 요약하기 (Paraphrasing)	
Step 4	**R**ecite
	요약문 말로 설명하기

18 Read the passage and follow the directions. [4 points]

Conspiracy theories are morality tales based on archetypal narratives about right versus wrong, good versus evil. Providing "black and white" world views, they foster societal divisions between in-groups and out-groups by exacerbating intolerance against "the other" and delegitimising different voices as being part of the conspiracy. Extremist groups use conspiracy theories as a tool for recruitment and to advance their radical agendas exploiting uncertainties, fears, socioeconomic issues and mental health disorders amongst vulnerable people. In recent years, right-wing extremism has proven to be active and efficient in the dissemination of conspiracy theories aimed at targeting individuals or groups blamed to be responsible for the evil in society. Shielding the audience from the risk of being drawn into the conspiratorial labyrinth of these groups is crucial to push back the ability of conspiracy theorists in mobilising extremist action and violence.

Conspiracy theories are a global phenomenon affecting almost every field of human activity. The belief that complex historical or political events, especially when they lack a clear explanation by the competent authorities or by the scientific community, are the result of secret conspiracies controlled by a small cabal of powerful people with malevolent intents has become a mainstream phenomenon in society. Such theories can be seen as attempts to give meaning to distressing events, to disclose their ultimate causes, and to connect the dots with what one may perceive as anomalous, suspicious or unexplained. In some cases, they are harmless and can be considered as part of the democratic discussion. In many other cases, however, conspiracy theories may be associated with radical behaviour, racist views, authoritarian attitudes and extremist ideologies with a deeply negative impact on society.

Amongst the most serious consequences is the fact that conspiracy theories may enhance the appeal of extremist narratives (e.g. providing seductive "black and white" explanations of polarising events), erode the trust between people and governments (e.g. promoting the idea that governments are controlled by shadow elites), spread hate speech (e.g. identifying a definitive group or person as being culpable), demolish the respect for evidence (e.g. attacking experts and their knowledge without having the necessary competence to perform verifications), mobilise violence (e.g. identifying targets), and even cause death (e.g. inducing people to refuse vaccine protection through the antivaxxer propaganda).

The outbreak of the COVID-19 pandemic acted as a catalyst for conspiracy theories. Given that the virus is invisible, corresponding conspiracy beliefs flourished, as in every period of crisis. Extremist groups capitalised on the opportunity by offering simple solutions and answers to highly _____ issues with the aim to advance their agendas and recruit followers. In this scenario, right-wing extremist groups played a major role in spreading hatred towards Jews and Muslims as well as anti-elite, racist and anti-immigration sentiments.

Fill in the blank with the ONE most appropriate word from the passage. Second, explain how Conspiracy theories can be related to a morality narrative. Do NOT copy more than FOUR consecutive words from the passage.

NOTE

Step 1	Survey
Key Words	
Signal Words	
Step 2	**Reading**
Purpose	
Pattern of Organization	
Tone	
Main Idea	
Step 3	**Summary**
지문 요약하기 (Paraphrasing)	
Step 4	**Recite**
	요약문 말로 설명하기

19 Read the passage and follow the directions. [4 points]

Personality tests have become popular tools for assessing individuals in various settings, from employment to education. However, their effectiveness in truly gauging a person's potential is highly questionable. While these tests can provide insights into certain personality traits, they are fundamentally limited in predicting future success or growth.

First, personality tests are inherently subjective because they rely on self-reported data. When individuals take these tests, their responses are often influenced by their current mood, self-perception, or even their desire to project a certain image. For example, someone might answer questions in a way that they think is socially desirable or aligns with how they want to be perceived, rather than how they truly are. This subjectivity can lead to inaccurate results that do not reflect the individual's true personality or potential.

Second, personality tests tend to categorize individuals into specific types or traits, which oversimplifies the complexity of human behavior and potential. These tests often operate on the assumption that people's personalities are static and can be neatly boxed into predefined categories. However, human behavior is dynamic and context-dependent, meaning that people can grow, adapt, and change in response to different situations and environments. By pigeonholing individuals into fixed categories, personality tests fail to capture the full spectrum of human potential.

While personality tests may offer some insights into a person's traits, they are ultimately inadequate for assessing potential. Their reliance on subjective self-reports and their tendency to oversimplify human behavior make them poor predictors of future success or development. To truly understand and assess potential, it is essential to consider the dynamic and multifaceted nature of human beings, which personality tests fail to do.

Write a summary following the guidelines below.

Guidelines

- Summarize the above passage in ONE paragraph.
- Provide a topic sentence, two supporting ideas, and a concluding sentence based on the passage.
- Do NOT copy more than FOUR consecutive words from the passage.

NOTE

Step 1	**S**urvey
Key Words	
Signal Words	
Step 2	**R**eading
Purpose	
Pattern of Organization	
Tone	
Main Idea	
Step 3	**S**ummary
지문 요약하기 (Paraphrasing)	
Step 4	**R**ecite
요약문 말로 설명하기	

20 Read the passage and follow the directions. [4 points]

> Today we take for granted that we live among diverse communities of animals that feed on each other. Our ecosystems are structured by feeding relationships like killer whales eating seals, which eat squid, which feed on krill. These and other animals require oxygen to extract energy from their food. But that's not how life on Earth used to be.
>
> With an environment devoid of oxygen and high in methane, for much of its history Earth would not have been a welcoming place for animals. The earliest life forms we know of were microscopic organisms (microbes) that left signals of their presence in rocks about 3.7 billion years old. The signals consisted of a type of carbon molecule that is produced by living things.
>
> Evidence of _____ was also preserved in the hard structures ("stromatolites") they made, which date to 3.5 billion years ago. Stromatolites are created as sticky mats of microbes trap and bind sediments into layers. Minerals precipitate inside the layers, creating durable structures even as the microbes die off. Scientists study today's, rare living stromatolite reefs to better understand Earth's earliest life forms.
>
> When cyanobacteria evolved at least 2.4 billion years ago, they set the stage for a remarkable transformation. They became Earth's first photo-synthesizers, making food using water and the Sun's energy, and releasing oxygen as a result. This catalyzed a sudden, dramatic rise in oxygen, making the environment less hospitable for other microbes that could not tolerate oxygen.
>
> Evidence for this Great Oxidation Event is recorded in changes in seafloor rocks called Banded Iron Formations, or BIFs. When shallow water, enriched in oxygen, mixes with deep, iron-rich water, the iron reacts chemically with oxygen (it gets oxidized) and forms iron oxide minerals. These minerals sink down to the seafloor, forming dark, iron-rich layers in the rocks.
>
> After the initial pulse of oxygen, it stabilized at lower levels where it would remain for a couple billion years more. In fact, as cyanobacteria died and drifted down through the water, the decomposition of their bodies probably reduced oxygen levels. So, the ocean was still not a suitable environment for most lifeforms that need ample oxygen.

Fill in the blank with the ONE most appropriate word from the passage. Second, according to the passage what made the Great Oxidation Event possible?

___

NOTE

Step 1	Survey
Key Words	
Signal Words	
Step 2	**Reading**
Purpose	
Pattern of Organization	
Tone	
Main Idea	
Step 3	**Summary**
지문 요약하기 (Paraphrasing)	
Step 4	**Recite**
요약문 말로 설명하기	

21 Read the passage and follow the directions. [4 points]

Encountering Stoicism in one way or another is the easy part. Understanding and explaining exactly what it is, though, is the tricky part. Recognizing and seeing exactly how it's relevant today and how it can help you, is the challenging part. Fully grasping it and putting it into practice, is the ambitious part—that's where the gold is hidden.

What the Stoics taught and practiced in the era of gladiators fighting for their lives and Romans socializing in steaming baths is still remarkably applicable in the era of Game of Thrones and Facebook. The wisdom of this ancient philosophy is _____.

After many years of school and university, I was sick of reading academic books and papers and learning about stuff that didn't really teach me anything of real life value. So, literally the day after handing in my final paper, I left the country and started my seven months long travel around the world. I wanted to get away, see places and other cultures, but mainly I wanted to get to know myself so I'd know what I wanted to do with my life when I got back. That last part did not work out; however, I did figure out something else instead: "I somehow must have missed the class on how to live?!"

In fifteen and a half years of schooling, I learned math, physics, chemistry, biology, and a bunch of other stuff, except how to deal with challenging situations? How to face my fears and struggles? What to do about my depressive feelings? How to deal effectively with the death of my friend? What to do with my anger? How to be more confident? Nope, I must have missed all those classes. That, by the way, is exactly what schools of philosophy were all about in the ancient world, they taught you how to live. And even though these schools don't exist anymore, you and I and most people are in as much need of a philosophy that teaches us how to live as we ever were.

Long story short, I decided to invest in myself and learn how to live well. From all the wisdom I devoured in the following years, Stoic philosophy helped me the most, even though it didn't start on good terms. Before I knew much (anything) about the philosophy, I thought this must be the most boring thing on earth. I mean, after all, it's called Stoicism and not "Supermanism" or something else that would indicate it's worth studying. I gave it a shot anyway, got hooked, and since then I've been a voracious student and practitioner of Stoic philosophy, discovering its timeless relevance in guiding a meaningful life.

Fill in the blank with the ONE most appropriate word from the passage. Second, explain the main reason the author became a student and practitioner of Stoic philosophy. Do Not copy more than FOUR consecutive words from the passage.

NOTE

Step 1	**S**urvey
Key Words	
Signal Words	
Step 2	**R**eading
Purpose	
Pattern of Organization	
Tone	
Main Idea	
Step 3	**S**ummary
지문 요약하기 (Paraphrasing)	
Step 4	**R**ecite
	요약문 말로 설명하기

22 Read the passage and follow the directions. [4 points]

> Pest and pathogen populations evolve resistance to pesticides and antiobiotics. For example, in the last 80 years, in more than 500 insect species, almost 8000 cases of insecticide resistance have been reported to more than 300 compounds. Likewise, among more than 1700 bacteria species, tens of thousands of putative resistance alleles have been characterized, conferring resistance to more than 200 antibiotics. In principle, one way to manage resistance evolution would be to keep developing new xenobiotics.
>
> But that might not be sustainable. It currently takes about 10 years and $1 billion to develop a new antibiotic, and it has been several decades since new insecticide or herbicide modes of action were discovered. The fact is that we have been losing effective chemical controls of pest populations faster than we have replaced them. This is already taking a toll on public health and prosperity. It could become worse. For antibiotics, by one estimate, before 2050, antimicrobial resistance will have killed 2.4 million people in Europe, North America and Australia, and will cost the world economy $3.5 billion in losses per year. If sustainable development of novel xenobiotics is not feasible, how can we focus on the conservation of the ones we have?
>
> To be clear, in the field, one of the strongest predictors of xenobiotic resistance evolution is application intensity; effective xenobiotic conservation will undoubtedly entail using them more sparingly and shifting to more integrated pest management approaches. But that leaves the question of how, when we do use xenobiotics, we should vary their application over time and space so as to maximize their durability, and thus the time a pest population is under control. That is our focus here.

Supposing for simplicity's sake that we have just two pesticides, we have four main _____ strategies to consider: sequential application, periodic application, mosaic application, and combined application. Which strategy is best? The combined strategy, where instead of trying to delay resistance evolution by adding heterogeneity to the selective environment, we use both pesticides together to consistently apply the strongest selection possible, is often the best and the sequential strategy is often the worst. Taken at face value, when in doubt, managers should use a combined application strategy. Of course, that might not be economical; indeed, theoretical evaluations of resistance management strategies have seldom considered economics. In other words, what works best in theory might not be sustainable in practice.

Fill in the blank with the ONE most appropriate word from the passage. Second, what is the limitation of theoretical evaluations of resistance management strategies mentioned in the passage?

유희태 일반영어 ❷

NOTE

Step 1	**S**urvey
Key Words	
Signal Words	
Step 2	**R**eading
Purpose	
Pattern of Organization	
Tone	
Main Idea	
Step 3	**S**ummary
지문 요약하기 (Paraphrasing)	
Step 4	**R**ecite
	요약문 말로 설명하기

23 Read the passage and follow the directions. [4 points]

Human lifeways range from Australia to the Arctic; from climes with baking sun to freezing cold. In explaining how humans thrive across the varied ecologies of the globe, cultural evolutionary researchers appeal to cumulative cultural traditions. These traditions are taken to distinguish human culture and explain the many adaptive lifeways of the human species.

Only some cultural traditions—genealogies of cultural traits whose existence and form depend upon previously expressed traits—are cumulative, where modifications to their form and/or function are preserved over time. Simplifying for the sake of exposition, traits can be considered as organised (often hierarchical) templates for action. Modifications, then, are additions, alterations to, or replacements of template components. If we consider a trait responsible for producing a particular dish, for example, one can understand the substitution of kale for cabbage represents as a replacement of one behaviour with another, while adding another tier to a multi-tiered cake would involve repeating a behaviour at a more encompassing hierarchical level. Cumulative cultural traditions, then, are genealogies of traits—organised templates for action—whose _____ are preserved over time.

This rough and ready characterization provides the conceptual basis for accounts of cumulative culture in the cultural evolutionary literature. However, note that so characterised, a range of human and non-human animal traditions qualify as cumulative. New Caledonian crows(Corvus moneduloides), for instance, grub for food using tools. Some of these tools are manufactured, involving the repeated notching and tearing of pandan leaves. Importantly, there is evidence that this manufacturing process is both socially transmitted and cumulative, with spatial variation in notching and tearing behaviour providing a living record of the modifications made to the tradition. So, on the rough and ready schematic, this tool manufacturing would be a cumulative cultural tradition.

Nonetheless, within the comparative cognition and cultural evolutionary literature, there is an emphasis on exploring and explaining what is distinctive about human cumulative culture. Indeed, on one prevalent account, the advent of cumulative culture marks a turning point in evolutionary history; a "Rubicon" whose shores separate organisms dominated by biological evolution (animals) from those dominated by cultural evolution (humans).

Humans, but not other animals, have a cultural "ratchet"; a suite of life history traits, cognitive capabilities, and social scaffolds that support the improvement, complexification, and diversification of cultural traditions. Unsurprisingly then, when further developing the concept of cumulative culture, researchers often do so in ways that delineate the cultural traditions or capabilities of animals from humans and their hominin precursors.

Fill in the blank with the ONE most appropriate word from the passage. Second, what distinguishes human cumulative culture from that of non-human animals, according to the passage?

NOTE

Step 1	Survey
Key Words	
Signal Words	
Step 2	**Reading**
Purpose	
Pattern of Organization	
Tone	
Main Idea	
Step 3	**Summary**
지문 요약하기 (Paraphrasing)	
Step 4	**Recite**
	요약문 말로 설명하기

24 Read the passage and follow the directions. [4 points]

> The decision to drop atomic bombs on Japan in 1945 remains one of the most controversial and significant actions in modern history. This critical decision was driven by a complex mix of military, political, and strategic factors.
>
> One reason was Japan's unwillingness to surrender unconditionally. Japan wanted to keep their emperor and conduct their own war trials and did not want to be occupied by U.S. forces. However, the United States wanted unconditional surrender, which thus meant the continuation of the war. Japan refused to surrender after multiple firebombing campaigns such as the Bombing of Tokyo on March 9 - 10, 1945. The Bombing of Tokyo alone claimed tens of thousands of lives and is often cited as one of the most destructive acts of war in history. It looked increasingly likely that the United States would have to commit itself to a land invasion, which could have claimed many American lives. Instead, the atomic bomb served as a tool to bring the war in the Pacific to a close sooner.
>
> Another reason why the United States dropped the atomic bombs—and, specifically, the second one on Nagasaki—has to do with the Soviet Union. On August 8, 1945, two days after the Hiroshima bombing, as agreed to by Joseph Stalin during the Tehrān and Yalta conferences in 1943 and 1945, respectively, the Soviet Union declared war on Japan. It is possible that U.S. President Harry Truman ordered the atomic bomb to be dropped on Nagasaki not only to further force Japan to surrender but also to keep the Soviets out of Japan by displaying American military power. Distrust and a sense of rivalry had been built up between the two superpowers that ultimately culminated in the Cold War.
>
> The decision to drop atomic bombs on Japan highlights the devastating consequences of warfare and the complex interplay of political and military strategies. This historical event serves as a stark reminder of the need for diplomatic efforts and international cooperation to prevent such catastrophic conflicts in the future.

Write a summary following the guidelines below.

Guidelines
• Summarize the above passage in ONE paragraph.
• Provide a topic sentence, two supporting ideas, and a concluding sentence based on the passage.
• Do NOT copy more than FOUR consecutive words from the passage.

NOTE

Step 1	**S**urvey
Key Words	
Signal Words	
Step 2	**R**eading
Purpose	
Pattern of Organization	
Tone	
Main Idea	
Step 3	**S**ummary
지문 요약하기 (Paraphrasing)	
Step 4	**R**ecite
	요약문 말로 설명하기

25 Read the passage and follow the directions. [4 points]

> People often cut in line: "May I use the Xerox machine?"—enabled them to cut 60% of the time. Adding that they were rushed allowed them to cut 94% of the time. And "May I use the Xerox machine, because I need to make copies?" was almost as effective, despite its flimsiness.
>
> The person directly behind an intrusion usually gets to decide whether to allow it. If that person doesn't object, other queuers tend to stay quiet.
>
> A person cutting in line has a 54% chance that others in the line will object. With two people cutting in line, there is a 91.3% chance that someone will object. The proportion of people objecting from anywhere behind the cutter is 73.3%, with the person immediately behind the point of intrusion objecting most frequently. Nevertheless, physical altercation resulting from cutting is rare.
>
> Some passengers who do not normally use a wheelchair request one, to pass through security checks quickly and to be among the first to board an aircraft. At the conclusion of the flight, these passengers walk off the aircraft, instead of waiting for a wheelchair and thus being among the last to disembark.
>
> Why do people let others cut in line? The main explanation I can find offered are that people are nice to those with stronger needs:
>
> Experimenters equipped with small bills approached 500 people in lines and offered a cash payment of up to $10 to cut in. Line-holders allowed the person to cut in but most wouldn't accept the money in return. The researchers took this to mean that people will allow cuts if they perceive the queue jumper has a real need to save time.
>
> When customers play the game just once, the only possible priority rule that can emerge is first in, first out; cut-ins must be rejected. But when players engage in repeated games, the pattern changes. Individuals in the line give way to those who appear to have more urgent needs or will require only a minimum of service time.

This all seems to me more likely an example of hidden motives. While we like to claim that we are being nice, I suggest that we are avoiding confrontation. When someone makes an apparently aggressive move at our expense, we can either oppose them and risk a confrontation, or give in and avoid confrontation. Giving in is much easier for us when we have the excuse of how doing so is in fact us being nice.

We all somehow seem to embrace the norm that those willing to risk confrontation should get their way, even if at others' expense. We accept the dominance of the willing to try to dominate.

What does the writer of the passage suggest is the real reason people let others cut in line? Second, explain how society's passive acceptance of aggressive behaviors contributes to the reinforcement of unfair power dynamics. Do NOT copy more than FOUR consecutive words from the passage.

NOTE

Step 1	Survey
Key Words	
Signal Words	
Step 2	**Reading**
Purpose	
Pattern of Organization	
Tone	
Main Idea	
Step 3	**Summary**
지문 요약하기 (Paraphrasing)	
Step 4	**Recite**
	요약문 말로 설명하기

26 Read the passage and follow the directions. [4 points]

It's a story that's become all too familiar—high winds knock out a power line, and a community can go without power for hours to days, an inconvenience at best and a dangerous situation at worst. UC Santa Cruz Professor Yu Zhang and his lab are leveraging tools to improve the efficiency, reliability, and resilience of power systems, and have developed an artificial intelligence (AI)-based approach for the smart control of microgrids for power restoration when outages occur.

They describe their new AI model and show that it outperforms traditional power restoration techniques. Nowadays, microgrids are the thing that both people in industry and in academia are focusing on for the future power distribution systems.

In many communities, infrastructure and its users are totally reliant on a local power generating utility company for electricity. This means that in the case of a disaster or extreme weather event, or even just a tree falling on a line, power goes out until repairs can be made. Today, many electricity systems are smart in that they are interconnected with computers and sensors. They often incorporate local renewable energy sources such as rooftop solar panels or small wind turbines, and some households and buildings rely on backup generators and/or energy batteries for their electricity demand.

This mix of power sources presents an opportunity to address outages locally by using alternative energy sources to provide electricity before upstream power is restored. One way to do this is with a microgrid, which distributes electricity to small areas such as a few buildings or a town— although the size of the microgrid can vary.

The microgrid can be connected to the main power utility source, but also can function while disconnected in "islanding mode," self-supported by alternate energy sources and unaffected by the issues impacting the main utility. Zhang's research team focuses on optimizing how microgrids pull from these various alternate sources such as renewables, generators, and batteries to restore power quickly and correctly.

> Zhang said that essentially they want to bring the power generation closer to the demand side in order to get rid of the long transmission lines. This could improve the power quality and reduce the power losses over the lines. In this way, "we will make the grid smaller, but stronger and more resilient."

What are the potential drawbacks of relying solely on traditional power restoration techniques during widespread power outages? Second, explain why microgrids are important for future power distribution systems. Do NOT copy more than FOUR consecutive words from the passage.

_____

_____

_____

_____

NOTE

Step 1	**S**urvey
Key Words	
Signal Words	
Step 2	**R**eading
Purpose	
Pattern of Organization	
Tone	
Main Idea	
Step 3	**S**ummary
지문 요약하기 (Paraphrasing)	
Step 4	**R**ecite
	요약문 말로 설명하기

27 Read the passage and follow the directions. [4 points]

> When referring to a "person of outlier," it's often in the context of someone who exhibits qualities, achievements, or behaviors that significantly deviate from the norm within their field or society. These individuals can be innovators, high achievers, or those whose characteristics are on the extreme ends of the spectrum. Just like outliers in data, people who are considered outliers can have both positive and negative impacts on their environment and themselves.
>
> Outliers often drive innovation because they think and act outside the conventional norms. Their unique perspectives and willingness to take risks can lead to groundbreaking discoveries, inventions, and artistic expressions. In addition, having individuals who think and act differently enriches a community or field of study by introducing a wide range of perspectives and solutions. This diversity of thought can lead to more robust discussions, decisions, and outcomes.
>
> Being significantly different can sometimes lead to feelings of isolation. Outliers may struggle to find peers who share their interests or understand their perspectives, potentially leading to loneliness or a sense of not belonging. Also, people who are outliers may be misunderstood by the majority, who may view their ideas or behaviors as eccentric or radical. This can lead to conflict, misinterpretation of intentions, and sometimes even social or professional repercussions.
>
> Being an outlier can be a double-edged sword. The unique attributes and capabilities of outliers can lead to significant contributions to society and personal fulfillment. However, the challenges they face highlight the importance of creating supportive environments that recognize and nurture diversity in all its forms. Encouragingly, as societies and institutions become more aware of the value of diversity and inclusion, the potential for outliers to thrive and positively impact the world increases.

Write a summary following the guidelines below.

── Guidelines ──
- Summarize the above passage in ONE paragraph.
- Provide a topic sentence, two supporting ideas, and a concluding sentence based on the passage.
- Do NOT copy more than FOUR consecutive words from the passage.

NOTE

Step 1	**S**urvey
Key Words	
Signal Words	
Step 2	**R**eading
Purpose	
Pattern of Organization	
Tone	
Main Idea	
Step 3	**S**ummary
지문 요약하기 (Paraphrasing)	
Step 4	**R**ecite
	요약문 말로 설명하기

28 Read the passage and follow the directions. [4 points]

> In 1917 a pivotal event occurred for art and philosophy: Marcel Duchamp unveiled his artwork *Fountain* in Alfred Stieglitz's New York studio. This was simply a porcelain urinal, signed 'R. Mutt'.
>
> *Fountain* was notorious, even for avant-garde artists. It has become one of the most discussed works of art of the 20th century. The Society of Independent Artists rejected it, though every artist who paid the exhibition fee was supposed to have their work shown. For almost a century, it has remained a difficult artwork. The philosopher John Passmore summed up *Fountain* as: 'a piece of mischief at the expense of the art world', though many have taken it very seriously.
>
> No doubt there was some tomfoolery involved—Duchamp did not choose a urinal randomly. Yet there is more to *Fountain* than nose-thumbing. What makes this artwork so striking is its philosophical contribution.
>
> Commentators often highlight the influence of *Fountain* on conceptual art, and this most 'aggressive' readymade has certainly had an enduring legacy. In 2004, it was voted the most important 20th-century work by hundreds of art experts. From Andy Warhol to Joseph Beuys to Tracey Emin, this urinal inspired artists to reconsider the traditional artwork. Instead of paintings and sculptures, art was suddenly Brillo boxes, an unmade bed, or a light-bulb plugged into a lemon: ordinary objects, some readymade, removed from their original contexts and placed on display in art galleries. The art critic Roberta Smith sums it up this way: 'Duchamp reduced the creative act to a stunningly rudimentary level: to the single, intellectual, largely random decision to name this or that object or activity "art".' Duchamp's choice was not random at all, but Smith's description points to the broader shock that Duchamp's work prompted: if this can be art, then anything can.

Since then, scholars have discussed *Fountain* to demonstrate a shift away from aesthetics to thought. As the philosopher Noël Carroll notes, it's possible to enjoy thinking about Duchamp's work without actually looking at it, which cannot be said for Henri Matisse's vivid paintings or Barbara Hepworth's dignified stone sculptures.

These traditional ideas are all important to *Fountain*. But they do not go far enough. They treat *Fountain* as art, but of a mocking sort: a kind of intellectual heckling that nudged artists to taunt and scoff more academically at their own field. Our explanation of the artwork's power is much more controversial: we believe that *Fountain* is art only insofar as it is not art. It is what it is not—and this is why it is what it is. In other words, the artwork delivers a true contradiction, what's called a dialetheia. *Fountain* did not simply usher in conceptual art—it afforded us an unusual and intriguing concept to consider: a work of art that isn't really a work of art, an everyday object that is not just an everyday object.

What can be inferred about the traits of "avant-garde artists" from the passage? Second, explain why the writer says "they do not go far enough". Do NOT copy more than FOUR consecutive words from the passage.

_____
_____
_____
_____

NOTE

Step 1	Survey
Key Words	
Signal Words	
Step 2	**Reading**
Purpose	
Pattern of Organization	
Tone	
Main Idea	
Step 3	**Summary**
지문 요약하기 (Paraphrasing)	
Step 4	**Recite**
	요약문 말로 설명하기

29 Read the passage and follow the directions. [4 points]

When we say 'marketing is broken' what do we mean? Simply, that it no longer does its job. Marketing is orientated around sales. If it doesn't initiate, assist or close a sale then it is failing. And failing it is. The largest single item on most firms' marketing spend is advertising, accounting for between a quarter and three-quarters of budgets. In some industries, marketing accounts for a third of revenues. Yet the link between marketing and consequential revenues is rarely demonstrable. Astonishing.

Marketing is based on notions that are 20 years out of date. The notion that if you put enough messages out there some of them will be heard. The notion that 'building the brand' is money well spent. The notion that people believe what they see and read. Recent initiatives to take advantage of Web 2.0 technologies are merely reactions that apply old techniques to new media. Marketing needs to rethink the messages it is communicating, to whom it's communicated and the methods being used. Many companies are disappointed at the lack of tangible _____ on their multi-million pounds marketing activities. Advertising remains the largest budget item on most firms' marketing plans. Advertising may be a fixture in a company's annual spend, but management boards are increasingly questioning why this is.

There is no strong evidence to suggest that advertising has any effect on sales. The academic research on marketing and return on investment (ROI) is paltry in number and unconvincing in conclusion. There is an awful lot of assertion from the profession itself, and several claims to the link between brand and revenues or stock price. It is true that firms with big revenues and profits usually have well-known brands. Yet brand awareness could equally be an outcome of high sales, rather than a driver of it. Google has never advertised, yet it has become the world's most powerful brand.

There exists in most companies a disconnect between sales and marketing. This manifests itself at an operational level in departmental warfare where sales forces and marketers feud like Capulets and Montagues—with disastrous results. Inside almost every company there lies a gulf between marketing and sales. Rarely is there harmony, at best just <u>an agreement to silently walk past on opposite sides of the corridor</u>. At worst, it can totally paralyse an organisation. Separate territories, with neither able to see the other's viewpoint.

Fill in the blank with the ONE most appropriate word from the passage. Second, describe to what the underlined "an agreement to silently walk past on opposite sides of the corridor" refers.

NOTE

Step 1	Survey
Key Words	
Signal Words	
Step 2	**Reading**
Purpose	
Pattern of Organization	
Tone	
Main Idea	
Step 3	**Summary**
지문 요약하기 (Paraphrasing)	
Step 4	**Recite**
	요약문 말로 설명하기

30 Read the passage and follow the directions. [4 points]

> Lily knows that Canberra is the capital of Australia. Aroha knows how to play the violin. What, if anything, do these "knowings" have in common? Traditionally philosophers have sharply distinguished knowings such as Lily's, that can seemingly be encapsulated and transmitted in propositions ("knowing-that"), from knowings such as Aroha's, that seem at least partly held in the body ("knowing-how"). Within such a framework, knowing-that has tended to be privileged as the sole and proper domain of epistemology and philosophy of mind, due to its supposed immediacy (under certain assumptions about the mind), and its clear interface with reasoning technologies such as speaking, writing and formal logic.
>
> Although this distinction goes back to Aristotle, it drew considerable strength from Descartes' metaphysical cleavage of mind from body in an attempt to establish indubitable knowledge. This led to understandings of knowing in terms of disembodied ideas or "propositions in the head" (today often referred to as "mental content"). This metaphor of the proposition in the head produces the key intellectualist idea that mindedness consists primarily in representing the world, rather than, say, transacting or coping with it. This focus on representation has further entrenched philosophers' tendency to treat even the most sophisticated "knowing-how" as not knowledge proper, but "mere" bodily skill. The cultural effects of this in downgrading our embodied experience have arguably been profound, both reflecting and also contributing to a socio-economic division of labour characteristic of modernity.

Phenomenology and pragmatism both evolved at least in part through critiquing intellectualism. Husserl, a famous phenomenologist, made this cultural and political point in polemical terms in his *Crisis of the European Sciences and Transcendental Phenomenology*, suggesting that intellectualist understandings of reason and rationality had produced a crisis of justification—for philosophy, the natural and human sciences, and our culture. Also, pragmatism rejects _____ because it neglects the role of agency in structuring meaning. As John Dewey famously noted, we are not just "spectators" (that is, representers) of reality, we also "intervene," and this should be included in the very notion of experience.

Fill in the blank with the ONE most appropriate word from the passage. Second, how does the intellectualist focus on "knowing-that" contribute to the socio-economic division of labor? Do NOT copy more than FOUR consecutive words from the passage.

NOTE

Step 1	**S**urvey
Key Words	
Signal Words	
Step 2	**R**eading
Purpose	
Pattern of Organization	
Tone	
Main Idea	
Step 3	**S**ummary
지문 요약하기 (Paraphrasing)	
Step 4	**R**ecite
	요약문 말로 설명하기

31 Read the passage and follow the directions. [4 points]

> The term forest fragmentation is often used to summarize the landscape-level structural changes to the forest exerted by a range of human activities. It is a process by which large and contiguous forests are divided into smaller patches due to human activities like agriculture, urban development, and infrastructure expansion. It poses significant environmental challenges. As forested areas become increasingly fragmented, the ecological integrity of these regions deteriorates, leading to various negative consequences.
>
> One major drawback of forest fragmentation is the loss of biodiversity. When forests are broken into smaller patches, habitats are reduced in size, and species that require large, continuous habitats may face extinction. Fragmentation also disrupts migration and breeding patterns, isolates populations, and increases the likelihood of inbreeding, which can further diminish genetic diversity. And the edges of these fragmented forests, often more exposed to external influences like invasive species, pollution, and climate change, are particularly vulnerable.
>
> Another significant consequence of forest fragmentation is its impact on ecosystem services. Forests are essential for carbon sequestration, soil conservation, and water regulation but fragmentation weakens these functions by reducing forest cover and disrupting the natural processes that sustain them. As a result, smaller forest patches become less effective at storing carbon, which worsens climate change. Additionally, fragmentation increases soil erosion and compromises water quality by disrupting the filtration processes typically provided by larger, intact forests.
>
> Forest fragmentation poses severe risks to biodiversity and the provision of ecosystem services. To mitigate these impacts, it is essential to prioritize conservation efforts that focus on preserving large, contiguous forest areas and restoring connectivity between fragmented habitats.

Write a summary following the guidelines below.

Guidelines

- Summarize the above passage in ONE paragraph.
- Provide a topic sentence, two supporting ideas, and a concluding sentence based on the passage.
- Do NOT copy more than FOUR consecutive words from the passage.

NOTE

Step 1	**S**urvey
Key Words	
Signal Words	
Step 2	**R**eading
Purpose	
Pattern of Organization	
Tone	
Main Idea	
Step 3	**S**ummary
지문 요약하기 (Paraphrasing)	
Step 4	**R**ecite
	요약문 말로 설명하기

32 Read the passage and follow the directions. [4 points]

University of Maryland researchers aiming to combat rising global temperatures have developed a new "cooling glass" that can turn down the heat indoors without electricity by drawing on the cold depths of space. The new technology, a microporous glass coating described in a paper published in the journal *Science*, can lower the temperature of the material beneath it by 3.5 degrees Celsius at noon, and has the potential to reduce a mid-rise apartment building's yearly carbon emissions by 10%.

The coating works in two ways: First, it reflects up to 99% of solar radiation to stop buildings from absorbing heat. More intriguingly, it emits heat in the form of longwave infrared radiation into the icy universe, where the temperature is generally around -270 degrees Celsius, or just a few degrees above absolute zero. In a phenomenon known as "radiative cooling," space effectively acts as a heat sink for the buildings; they take advantage of the new cooling glass design along with the so-called atmospheric transparency window—a part of the electromagnetic spectrum that passes through the atmosphere without boosting its temperature—to dump large amounts of _____ into the infinite cold sky beyond.

"It's a game-changing technology that simplifies how we keep buildings cool and energy-efficient," said Assistant Research Scientist Xinpeng Zhao, the first author of the study. "This could change the way we live and help us take better care of our home and our planet." Unlike previous attempts at cooling coatings, the new UMD-developed glass is environmentally stable—able to withstand exposure to water, ultraviolet radiation, dirt and even flames, enduring temperatures of up to 1,000 degrees Celsius. The glass can be applied to a variety of surfaces like tile, brick and metal, making the technology highly scalable and adoptable for wide use.

The team used finely ground glass particles as a binder, allowing them to avoid polymers and enhance its long-term durability outdoors. And they chose the particle size to maximize emission of infrared heat while simultaneously reflecting sunlight. The development of the cooling glass aligns with global efforts to cut energy consumption and fight climate change. The cooling glass is more than a new material—it's a key part of the solution to climate change. By cutting down on air conditioning use, we're taking big steps toward using less energy and reducing our carbon footprint. It shows how new technology can help us build a cooler, greener world.

Fill in the blank with the ONE most appropriate word from the passage. Second, how does the development of the cooling glass align with global efforts to combat climate change? Do NOT copy more than FOUR consecutive words from the passage.

NOTE

Step 1	Survey
Key Words	
Signal Words	
Step 2	**Reading**
Purpose	
Pattern of Organization	
Tone	
Main Idea	
Step 3	**Summary**
지문 요약하기 (Paraphrasing)	
Step 4	**Recite**
	요약문 말로 설명하기

33 Read the passage and follow the directions. [4 points]

What was once a routine way to pay your bills—handwriting paper checks at the kitchen table, dropping envelopes into a blue metal box on the street—has become a high-risk endeavor: It provides the raw materials for low-level fraud artists and sophisticated crime rings, costing financial institutions billions. It has put banks on high alert, though their efforts to catch the fraud also routinely entangles innocent customers, causing institutions to suddenly freeze or shut down customer accounts in the process. Many fraudsters manage to disappear without any consequences.

Even as check usage has rapidly declined over the past couple of decades, check fraud has risen sharply, particularly since the pandemic. The cons may start with stealing pieces of paper, but they leverage technology and social media to commit fraud on a grander scale, banking insiders and fraud experts said. In the past, criminals needed a special internet browser that would grant entry into the dark web marketplace of _____ checks, maybe even someone to vouch for them. Now all they need is an account from Telegram, a messaging app.

"You can buy checks on the internet for $45, with a perfectly good signature," said John Ravita, director of business development at SQN Banking Systems, which provides check fraud detection software. "There is one website that offers a money-back guarantee. It's like Nordstrom."

A recent surge in mail theft caused the Financial Crimes Enforcement Network—an arm of the Treasury Department known as FinCEN that is charged with safeguarding the financial system—to sound alarm bells this year. Thieves have attacked mail carriers or stolen and sold carriers' arrow keys, which unlock mailboxes within a certain area. The checks are stolen from the mail, and then criminals carry out a classic fraud: "washing" the checks using something as basic as nail polish remover, leaving the signature untouched. Others "cook" new checks by scanning and altering the old ones.

> Some criminals deposit checks into their own accounts, while others list them for sale. But the schemes have grown sophisticated. Not only can thieves buy stolen checks; they can purchase bank accounts in which to deposit them, along with the mobile phone number and device used to create that account, among other things.

Fill in the blank with the ONE most appropriate word from the passage. Second, how have the methods used in check fraud become more advanced in recent years? Do NOT copy more than FOUR consecutive words from the passage.

NOTE

Step 1	**S**urvey
Key Words	
Signal Words	
Step 2	**R**eading
Purpose	
Pattern of Organization	
Tone	
Main Idea	
Step 3	**S**ummary
지문 요약하기 (Paraphrasing)	
Step 4	**R**ecite
	요약문 말로 설명하기

34 Read the passage and follow the directions. [4 points]

> There is a growing trend toward applying quantum mechanics, a science for studying microscopic particles such as protons and electrons, in computing, communication, and sensing. Quantum computing is an interdisciplinary field that seeks to understand the processing and transmission of information using quantum mechanics principles. Quantum computing is the exploitation of properties of quantum states such as superposition and entanglement to perform computation. The devices that perform quantum computations are called quantum computers. Quantum technologies are creating a massive paradigm shift in computing technology. Today the main industry trends, including Industry 4.0, have incorporated the digital revolution into the physical world, meanwhile promoting new technologies such as artificial intelligence, quantum computing, and nanotechnology. One of the drivers of the Industry 4.0 could be quantum computing, which harnesses quantum mechanical concepts such as superposition and entanglement to perform computation, although a full-scale quantum computer has not yet been developed.
>
> Quantum technologies have been under development worldwide for more than 20 years, resulting in promising results and progress. The main research subject of quantum technology is the interdisciplinary subject of quantum mechanics and Information and Communication Technology (ICT). Quantum information technology is a multidisciplinary field that seeks to understand the processing and transmission of information using quantum mechanics principles. It includes theoretical research and experimental study in quantum physics and computations. It combines quantum effects in physics with ICT. Now quantum information technology is considered a frontier technology that combines quantum physics and ICT. It has been rapidly developed into an emerging interdisciplinary subject mainly based on the fundamental principles of quantum mechanics and ICT.

In _____ computing, the bit is the basic unit of information in computing and communications. The bit represents a logical state with one of two possible values. These values are represented as either "1" or "0". Conventional computing technologies adopt bits of 0 and 1, and the computation is facilitated by bits. Quantum computing is a new paradigm that uses quantum theory to replace current computing. Quantum computing exploits the collective properties of quantum states to perform computation. Quantum computing can process more data than conventional data consisting of 0 and 1.

As mentioned above, a bit would have to be in one state or the other in a conventional system. A qubit or quantum bit is the basic unit of quantum information in quantum computing. Quantum mechanics allows the qubit to be in a coherent superposition of both states simultaneously, a fundamental property of quantum mechanics and quantum computing. Quantum computers use quantum superposition to process information in parallel, which provides a fundamental computing advantage over conventional computers.

Fill in the blank with the ONE most appropriate word from the passage. Second, what specific two factors make quantum computing superior to conventional computing?

NOTE

Step 1	Survey
Key Words	
Signal Words	
Step 2	**Reading**
Purpose	
Pattern of Organization	
Tone	
Main Idea	
Step 3	**Summary**
지문 요약하기 (Paraphrasing)	
Step 4	**Recite**
	요약문 말로 설명하기

35 Read the passage and follow the directions. [4 points]

Digital humanities, a field at the intersection of computing and the disciplines of the humanities, encompasses a wide range of activities and approaches. Among these, two primary types stand out. Each represents a distinct application of technology in the service of humanistic inquiry, offering unique benefits.

The first type, computational analysis, involves using algorithms and data processing techniques to analyze large sets of textual, visual, or auditory data. This approach allows scholars to uncover patterns and insights that would be impossible to detect manually. For example, text mining and natural language processing can reveal thematic trends in literature across different periods, or social network analysis can trace connections and influences among historical figures. Computational analysis thus opens new avenues for research, enabling scholars to ask and answer questions at a scale and granularity previously unimaginable.

The second type, digital archiving, focuses on the preservation and accessibility of cultural artifacts in digital formats. This includes digitizing manuscripts, artworks, and other materials, and creating online repositories where these resources can be accessed globally. Digital archives make it possible to preserve fragile or rare items, democratizing access to information and fostering global scholarly collaboration. An example of this is the digitization of the Dead Sea Scrolls, which allows researchers worldwide to study these ancient texts without the need to travel.

Computational analysis and digital archiving represent two fundamental types of digital humanities, each contributing to the field in significant ways. Computational analysis leverages technology to enhance research capabilities, while digital archiving ensures the preservation and accessibility of cultural heritage. Together, these approaches enrich the humanities, offering new tools and methods for exploring the human experience. As technology continues to evolve, the potential for digital humanities to transform scholarship will only grow, underscoring the importance of these two types in the broader academic landscape.

Write a summary following the guidelines below.

── Guidelines ──
- Summarize the above passage in ONE paragraph.
- Provide a topic sentence, two supporting ideas, and a concluding sentence based on the passage.
- Do NOT copy more than FOUR consecutive words from the passage.

NOTE

Step 1	Survey
Key Words	
Signal Words	
Step 2	**Reading**
Purpose	
Pattern of Organization	
Tone	
Main Idea	
Step 3	**Summary**
지문 요약하기 (Paraphrasing)	
Step 4	**Recite**
	요약문 말로 설명하기

36 Read the passage and follow the directions. [4 points]

Angie Xue had always wanted to travel to Korea, so when she saw that $600 round-trip flights were available from California, she booked one immediately. "It was now or never," she recalls via phone. Xue's first order of planning after that? Booking a personal color analysis appointment in Seoul, something she'd discovered through viral videos.

Personal color analysis aims to assign individuals flattering colors that can inform their choices around clothing, makeup and accessories based on their complexions and skin tones. The process can take 60 minutes, with color consultants draping hundreds of fabric swatches across clients' shoulders to carefully examine what makes their faces light up rather than emphasize dark circles or wrinkles.

For decades it's been used by politicians, chief executive officers and the social elite as a way to put their best feet forward. Now, on the heels of a TikTok craze, it's sprouting up from California to New York, and Gen Z loyalists are increasingly making trips to Seoul with the procedure topping their bucket list.

In the U.S., a three-hour-long session at a place like House of Colour in Brooklyn, New York, can cost $545; in most Korean studios, the rates hover from $80 to $160. The trick is getting an appointment, particularly in Seoul. In her quest, Xue called more than 30 places before managing to book slots for herself and her boyfriend. But because her color consultant didn't speak English, she was warned, she had to spend an additional $50 per hour to hire a translator.

The craze around personal color was booming before Covid-19 hit South Korea. Now it's resurging along with international visitation. During Covid, a lot of foreigners watched K-dramas and Korean movies and personal color was often talked about in the shows, so it became a big interest to foreigners.

Color analysis has undoubtedly been having a pop culture moment. A simple site search of "Personal Color Analysis Korea" shows the topic has 375 million TikTok views, with content creators posting their experience, including detailed step-by-step instructions on how to book the service and where to go. A viral video in which Jisoo, a member of smash K-pop group Blackpink, details her personal color analysis results has garnered 2.6 million views on YouTube alone.

Personal color analysis has become a big part of _____ in Korea. Possibly if you don't know what your personal color is, it's hard to shop for the appropriate makeup and clothing—and to also converse with the younger generation.

Fill in the blank with the ONE most appropriate word from the passage. Second, explain what the purpose of personal color analysis is. Do NOT copy more than FOUR consecutive words from the passage.

_____
_____
_____
_____

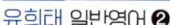

Step 1	**S**urvey
Key Words	
Signal Words	
Step 2	**R**eading
Purpose	
Pattern of Organization	
Tone	
Main Idea	
Step 3	**S**ummary
지문 요약하기 (Paraphrasing)	
Step 4	**R**ecite
요약문 말로 설명하기	

37 Read the passage and follow the directions. [4 points]

> This is the happiest story you've ever read. It's about two people who led wonderfully fulfilling lives. They had engrossing careers, earned the respect of their friends, and made important contributions to their neighborhood, their country, and their world. And the odd thing was, they weren't born geniuses. They did okay on the SAT and IQ tests and that sort of thing, but they had no extraordinary physical or mental gifts. They were fine-looking, but they weren't beautiful. Yet they achieved this success, and everyone who met them sensed that they lived blessed lives.
>
> How did they do it? They possessed what economists call noncognitive skills, which is the catchall category for hidden qualities that can't be easily counted or measured, but which in real life lead to happiness and fulfillment.
>
> First, they had good character. They were energetic, honest, and dependable. They were persistent after setbacks and acknowledged their mistakes. They possessed enough confidence to take risks and enough integrity to live up to their commitments. They tried to recognize their weaknesses, atone for their sins, and control their worst impulses.
>
> Just as important, they had _____. They knew how to read people, situations, and ideas. You could put them in front of a crowd, or bury them with a bunch of reports, and they could develop an intuitive feel for the landscape before them—what could go together and what would never go together, what course would be fruitful and what would never be fruitful. The skills a master seaman has to navigate the oceans, they had to navigate the world.

Over the centuries, zillions of books have been written about how to succeed. But these tales are usually told on the surface level of life. They describe the colleges people get into, the professional skills they acquire, the conscious decisions they make, and the tips and techniques they adopt to build connections and get ahead. These books often focus on an outer definition of success, having to do with IQ, wealth, prestige, and worldly accomplishments. This story is told one level down. This success story emphasizes the role of the inner mind—the unconscious realm of emotions, intuitions, biases, longings, genetic predispositions, character traits, and social norms.

This is the realm where character is formed and street smarts grow. We are living in the middle of a revolution in consciousness. Over the past few years, geneticists, neuroscientists, psychologists, sociologists, economists, anthropologists, and others have made great strides in understanding the building blocks of human flourishing. And a core finding of their work is that we are not primarily the products of our conscious thinking. We are primarily the products of thinking that happens below the level of awareness.

Fill in the blank with the TWO most appropriate consecutive words from the passage. Second, identify the TWO consecutive words from the passage that best correspond to the meaning of the underlined "thinking that happens below the level of awareness."

NOTE

Step 1	Survey
Key Words	
Signal Words	
Step 2	**Reading**
Purpose	
Pattern of Organization	
Tone	
Main Idea	
Step 3	**Summary**
지문 요약하기 (Paraphrasing)	
Step 4	**Recite**
	요약문 말로 설명하기

38 Read the passage and follow the directions. [4 points]

> Dr. Taraneh Nazem, a reproductive endocrinologist and infertility specialist for RMA of New York, recently watched a TikTok video claiming that eating raw cacao daily could completely balance your hormones and cure PMS. "The creator made sweeping statements without any scientific backing, and the comment section was filled with people eager to try it—despite cacao's known potential to cause insomnia and anxiety if consumed in large quantities," says Nazem.
>
> Social-media is rife with posts like this, pushing superfoods and supplements to boost your hormonal health and improve your low energy, poor sleep, bad acne, and so many other ills in the process. Every day, another influencer on TikTok claims that superfoods can change our hormonal balance. The myths that especially irk Nazem: apple cider vinegar helps women with PCOS, green tea is the secret to better insulin sensitivity, and butter supports healthy estrogen levels.
>
> Do you even need to "balance your hormones," as many on social-media tout in their hashtags? Experts share what foods can—and can't—do for your hormonal health.
>
> But a person's big-picture way of eating—not any single food included in their diet—is what can truly affect _____. An unhealthy diet high in processed foods and saturated fats can lead to conditions like metabolic syndrome, diabetes, and polycystic ovary syndrome [PCOS]. That's because a diet high in sweets, dairy, refined grains, red meat, and processed foods can raise estrogen levels and promote insulin resistance due to higher body fat.

It's also possible to have hormone-based medical issues that can be helped by a dietary overhaul. Kaytee Hadley, a functional dietitian, recently worked with a young woman experiencing unpleasant gut symptoms along with irregular cycles, PMS, and ovarian cysts, which would rupture regularly and cause excruciating pain. "It was clear she had hormonal imbalances," says Hadley. After running a few tests, it was also determined that she had nutritional deficiencies and poor gut health exacerbating these issues.

Hadley had the client focus on a "food-first approach" by adding more nourishment and gut-friendly foods, addressing her vitamin deficiencies, and developing a consistent eating schedule with foods she enjoyed. In less than six months, the client had no more symptoms of PMS or cysts, her acne cleared up, her cycles became more regular.

But this success story doesn't apply to the average person—and no "magic" superfood touted on TikTok can have these effects. It wasn't, say, the beans or tofu she started eating more regularly that "cured" her sex hormone imbalances, but sweeping lifestyle changes that focused on a healthy diet, exercise, stress-reduction techniques, and improving her sleep.

Fill in the blank with the TWO most appropriate consecutive words from the passage. Second, according to Kaytee Hadley, what approach did she use to help a client with hormonal imbalances?

NOTE

Step 1	Survey
Key Words	
Signal Words	
Step 2	**Reading**
Purpose	
Pattern of Organization	
Tone	
Main Idea	
Step 3	**Summary**
지문 요약하기 (Paraphrasing)	
Step 4	**Recite**
	요약문 말로 설명하기

39 Read the passage and follow the directions. [4 points]

The question of why human beings are violent has intrigued philosophers, psychologists, and anthropologists for centuries. Violence, whether on a personal or societal level, is a complex behavior influenced by a myriad of factors, both innate and environmental. Understanding these factors can help us better comprehend why violence persists in human society despite our advancements in civilization and morality.

Human violence is deeply rooted in our evolutionary history, where aggression was vital for survival. Early humans relied on aggression to defend themselves, secure resources, and establish social dominance, traits that have been passed down through generations. Although the contexts in which aggression manifests have evolved, these ingrained behaviors still influence modern human interactions. Psychological factors also contribute to violence. Mental health disorders, such as personality disorders, can predispose individuals to aggressive behavior, while intense emotions like anger and fear can trigger violent actions, especially in situations where individuals feel threatened or powerless.

Environmental influences further shape violent behavior. Early exposure to violence or neglect during childhood can foster aggressive tendencies that persist into adulthood. Societal factors, including cultural norms that glorify aggression, economic inequality, and political instability, also play critical roles in fostering violence. For instance, societies with high levels of inequality and fewer opportunities for peaceful conflict resolution are more likely to experience higher rates of violence.

Human violence is a multifaceted issue rooted in evolutionary history, shaped by social and environmental factors, and influenced by psychological states. Addressing violence requires a holistic approach that considers all these aspects, aiming to reduce both the causes and opportunities for violent behavior in society.

Write a summary following the guidelines below.

Guidelines

- Summarize the above passage in ONE paragraph.
- Provide a topic sentence, two supporting ideas, and a concluding sentence based on the passage.
- Do NOT copy more than FOUR consecutive words from the passage.

NOTE

Step 1	**S**urvey
Key Words	
Signal Words	
Step 2	**R**eading
Purpose	
Pattern of Organization	
Tone	
Main Idea	
Step 3	**S**ummary
지문 요약하기 (Paraphrasing)	
Step 4	**R**ecite
	요약문 말로 설명하기

40 Read the passage and follow the directions. [4 points]

Rejoicing in its busiest every year of visitors, Japan has begun to fret about overtourism. It is tangled on whether two-tier pricing, with one price for foreign visitors and a lower one for locals, is desirable, discriminatory or self-destructive. Rather than escaping it all, a once-footloose nation is opting to stay put, anchoring Japanese overseas travel at a mere 60 per cent of pre-Covid levels.

But somewhere in all this, the right crisis—one of negative terms of trade and currency vulnerability—has at last been identified. The run-up to this week's Bank of Japan monetary policy meeting was messy; but the message the central bank transmitted on the yen was clearer and more honest than it has been for a long time. For all the BoJ's reference to an intensifying virtuous cycle between wages and prices and its previous commitment to moving only if the data justified it, the decision to raise the benchmark interest rate to 0.25 per cent was hardly a no-brainer.

Two members of the monetary policy committee dissented, with one directly questioning whether the economic data yet supported an increase. Some analysts have already suggested Wednesday's move may be remembered as one of the BoJ's most controversial in recent times; the chief Japan economist at UBS described it as "very disappointing", warning that it made the already precarious normalisation of Japan's economy even more so.

And there are other, less neatly quantifiable signals of fragility—the tourism-related phenomena mentioned above prominent among them. On the collapse in Japanese overseas travel, many have identified the _____ yen (the worst-performing major currency in 2024 and at a 37-year low in June) as the central cause.

Similarly, the debate on two-tier pricing highlights another piece of unfinished economic business. Japan's multi-decade battle with deflation may be over, but pricing power in goods and services remains anaemic. Japan talks of higher costs for tourists as a policy issue because it still has not recovered the habit of pricing as the natural function of the market and, again, of confidence.

Finally, on overtourism, the Japanese grumbling is partially related to the weak yen—<u>there is a humiliation in hearing visitors from smaller economies revelling in how cheap everything feels</u>. But there is also frustration with the economics. If the Japanese had the money and security to enjoy their own country as freely as the visitors, the overcrowding would rankle less.

Fill in the blank with the ONE most appropriate word from the passage. Second, explain what the underlined "there is a humiliation in hearing visitors from smaller economies revelling in how cheap everything feels" means. Do Not copy more than FOUR consecutive words from the passage.

NOTE

Step 1	Survey
Key Words	
Signal Words	
Step 2	**Reading**
Purpose	
Pattern of Organization	
Tone	
Main Idea	
Step 3	**Summary**
지문 요약하기 (Paraphrasing)	
Step 4	**Recite**
	요약문 말로 설명하기

41 Read the passage and follow the directions. [4 points]

>   One of our great urbanists and one of our great public health experts join forces to reckon with how cities are changing in the face of existential threats the pandemic has only accelerated. Cities can make us sick. They always have—diseases spread more easily when more people are close to one another. And disease is hardly the only ill that accompanies urban density. Cities have been demonized as breeding grounds for vice and crime from Sodom and Gomorrah on. But cities have _____ nonetheless because they are humanity's greatest invention, indispensable engines for creativity, innovation, wealth, and connection, the loom on which the fabric of civilization is woven.
>
>   But cities now stand at a crossroads. During the global COVID crisis, cities grew silent as people worked from home—if they could work at all. The normal forms of socializing ground to a halt. How permanent are these changes? Advances in digital technology mean that many people can opt out of city life as never before. Will they? Are we on the brink of a post-urban world? City life will survive but individual cities face terrible risks and a wave of urban failure would be absolutely disastrous. In terms of intimacy and inspiration, nothing can replace what cities offer.
>
>   Great cities have always demanded great management, and our current crisis has exposed fearful gaps in our capacity for good governance. It is possible to drive a city into the ground, pandemic or not. Glaeser and Cutler examine the evolution that is already happening, and describe the possible futures that lie before us: What will set apart the cities that have flourished from those that have not? In America deep inequities in health care and education are a particular blight on the future of our cities. <u>Solving them will be the difference between our collective good health and a downward spiral to a much darker place.</u>

Fill in the blank with the ONE most appropriate word from the passage. Second, explain what the underlined "Solving them will be the difference between our collective good health and a downward spiral to a much darker place" means. Do NOT copy more than FOUR consecutive words from the passage.

_____
_____
_____

NOTE

Step 1	**S**urvey
Key Words	
Signal Words	
Step 2	**R**eading
Purpose	
Pattern of Organization	
Tone	
Main Idea	
Step 3	**S**ummary
지문 요약하기 (Paraphrasing)	
Step 4	**R**ecite
	요약문 말로 설명하기

42 Read the passage and follow the directions. [4 points]

> The problem would be a common experience of digital media overload and indications that online media or smartphone use is causing concern for individuals and institutions. Although it is difficult to determine the exact nature of the problem and how widespread it might be, indications of concern are found in numbers, in media texts and in discussion.
>
> Surveys and statistics from the world's internet-rich countries show that a substantial proportion expressly agrees to statements such as 'I use my phone too much'. Norway is a relevant case because it is one of the world's most digitally connected countries and studies of Nordic populations confirm a widespread sense of online overuse. However, surveys from large markets elsewhere indicate that such concerns are shared: in the UK and the US, between one third and half of the adult population say that they spend too much time on their phones.
>
> <u>Parallel to the growing numbers, media texts about offline measures proliferate</u>. According to the global news database *Factiva*, the first mention of digital detox was in 2006, but usage did not take off until 2010. In 2013, digital detox was added to the *Oxford online dictionary*, and that year saw a distinct increase in mentions. By mid-2019, the total number of entries on digital detox in the database was rapidly approaching 9,000. The UK tops the list of countries referring to it, followed by Germany, the US, Australia and India, while the most mentioned industries are, by far, smartphones and social media. Not surprisingly, Facebook is the most referenced company. Mentions also include other media and entertainment industries as well as digital detox hotels and tourism.

The numbers and texts reflect that overuse and restricting media use have become talking points. The topic is discussed in social media, blogs, family gatherings, schools and workplaces. New terms and aphorisms enrich our vocabularies. FOMO has emerged as shorthand for a new condition: Fear of Missing Out, a force presumably driving smartphone and social media use. JOMO is the opposite: Joy of Missing Out, what digital detoxers strive for, a sense of enjoying life here-and-now and not through a screen. Phubbing is shorthand for mobile phone snubbing: using the phone to shut someone out. Screen wall is another way to say the same, and screen time is emerging as a central object of negotiation in families. Already in 2008, the UK Post Office was cited as saying that 13 million Britons suffered from nomophobia—No Mobile Phobia, feeling stressed when their mobile was out of battery or lost. Digital detox is a new term but stands in a long tradition of using medical vocabulary to talk about media use.

Explain the relationship between the rise in digital overuse concerns and the increase in discussions about offline solutions, as suggested by the underlined part. Do NOT copy more than FOUR consecutive words from the passage. Second, explain why the writer mentions such terms as "FOMO", "JOMO" and "Phubbing" in the passage. Do NOT copy more than FOUR consecutive words from the passage.

NOTE

Step 1	Survey
Key Words	
Signal Words	
Step 2	**Reading**
Purpose	
Pattern of Organization	
Tone	
Main Idea	
Step 3	**Summary**
지문 요약하기 (Paraphrasing)	
Step 4	**Recite**
	요약문 말로 설명하기

43   Read the passage and follow the directions. [4 points]

Dolly Parton is credited with the phrase "the higher the hair, the closer to God," but King Louis XIV might have shared her sentiments some 300 years earlier. Wigs had been around for millennia in the Mediterranean and Europe.

Some of history's oldest wigs were donned by the elite of ancient Egypt, both in life and death. Wigs have been found on mummies' heads, and ancient tombs contain wig boxes along with other personal items. Later elite Romans wore fashionable wigs and wealthy women favored blond hair imported from Germany. England's Queen Elizabeth I (1558-1603) hid her thinning hair with a collection of more than 80 red wigs. The archaic term for wig, periwig, from the French perruque, made one of its earliest written appearances in the 1590s, in William Shakespeare's early play *The Two Gentlemen of Verona*.

These English roots would give way to French dominance by the mid-17th century, when the 23-year-old king of France went prematurely bald in 1624. Before his hair loss, King Louis XIII had worn his natural hair luxuriantly long, a sign of health and virility. Thinning hair and baldness had become associated with sickness, perhaps because those who suffered from syphilis were "treated" with mercury, whose toxic effects included hair loss. Louis XIII may have started the trend, but his successor, Louis XIV, would take it to new heights. The four-year-old king succeeded his father in 1643. As he grew, Louis XIV wore his brown hair in long, wavy curls. Louis XIV, in his 30s, gave up on half measures and wore a long, full-bottomed wig of tight curls.

Wigs have a rich history as symbols of status and fashion, evolving significantly over time. In light of this historical context, today's fascination with hair and fashion can draw inspiration from these rich traditions. Embracing modern alternatives, such as high-quality synthetic wigs or hair extensions, allows individuals to achieve similar status and style without the cumbersome weight and maintenance of historical wigs.

Write a summary following the guidelines below.

― Guidelines ―

- Summarize the above passage in ONE paragraph.
- Provide a topic sentence, two supporting ideas, and a concluding sentence based on the passage.
- Do NOT copy more than FOUR consecutive words from the passage.

NOTE

Step 1	Survey
Key Words	
Signal Words	
Step 2	**Reading**
Purpose	
Pattern of Organization	
Tone	
Main Idea	
Step 3	**Summary**
지문 요약하기 (Paraphrasing)	
Step 4	**Recite**
	요약문 말로 설명하기

44 Read the passage and follow the directions. [4 points]

Plato discusses love (erôs) and friendship (philia) primarily in two dialogues, the *Lysis* and the *Symposium*, though the *Phaedrus* also adds significantly to his views. In each work, Socrates as the quintessential philosopher is in two ways center stage, first, as a lover of wisdom (sophia) and discussion (logos), and, second, as himself an inverter or disturber of erotic norms. Plato's views on love are a meditation on Socrates and the power his philosophical conversations have to mesmerize, obsess, and educate.

"The only thing I say I know," Socrates tells us in the *Symposium*, "is the art of love". Taken literally, it is an incredible claim. Are we really to believe that the man who affirms when on trial for his life that he knows himself to be wise "in neither a great nor a small way" knows the art of love? In fact, the claim is a nontrivial play on words facilitated by the fact that the noun erôs ("love") and the verb erôtan ("to ask questions") sound as if they are etymologically connected. Socrates knows about the art of love in that—but just insofar as—he knows how to ask questions, how to converse elenctically.

Just how far that is, we discover in the *Lysis*, where Socrates makes a similar claim. Hippothales, like Socrates, loves beautiful boys and philosophical discussions. But he does not know the art of love and so does not know how to talk to Lysis—the boy with whom he is in love. What Hippothales does is sing eulogies to Lysis, and that, Socrates argues, no skilled lover would ever do. For if your suit succeeds "everything you've said and sung turns out to eulogize yourself as victor in having won such a boyfriend," but if it fails, then "the greater your praise of his beauty and goodness, the more you will seem to have lost and the more you will be ridiculed." Consequently, someone "who is wise in the art of love doesn't praise his beloved until he has him: he fears how the future may turn out". Convinced, Hippothales asks Socrates to tell him "what someone should say or do to get his prospective boyfriend to love him?". Socrates is uncharacteristically forthcoming: "if you're willing to have him talk with me, I might be able to give you a demonstration of how to carry on a discussion with him". What follows is an elenctic examination of Lysis. Socrates' lessons in love, we may infer, are elenctic lessons—lessons in how to ask and answer questions.

At the end of the examination, Socrates characterizes what he has accomplished: "This is how you should talk to your boyfriends, Hippothales, making them humble and <u>drawing in their sails, instead of swelling them up</u> and spoiling them, as you do". It sounds simply chastening put like that. But in the overall context of the *Lysis*, where love is a desire and desire is an emptiness, it is much more.

Explain what the underlined "drawing in their sails, instead of swelling them up" means. Second, explain why Socrates argues that singing eulogies to a beloved is not the proper way to demonstrate love, according to his discussion with Hippothales in Plato's *Lysis*. Do Not copy more than FOUR consecutive words from the passage.

NOTE

Step 1	**S**urvey
Key Words	
Signal Words	
Step 2	**R**eading
Purpose	
Pattern of Organization	
Tone	
Main Idea	
Step 3	**S**ummary
지문 요약하기 (Paraphrasing)	
Step 4	**R**ecite
	요약문 말로 설명하기

2S2R

유희태 일반영어 ② 유형

초판 1쇄	2014년 3월 13일	
2쇄	2014년 3월 29일	
2판 1쇄	2015년 2월 17일	저자와의
2쇄	2015년 2월 23일	협의하에
3쇄	2016년 2월 25일	인지생략
3판 1쇄	2017년 3월 10일	
2쇄	2018년 2월 20일	
3쇄	2018년 12월 15일	
4판 1쇄	2020년 2월 10일	
2쇄	2020년 12월 10일	
5판 1쇄	2022년 1월 10일	
2쇄	2023년 1월 5일	
3쇄	2024년 9월 5일	
6판 1쇄	2026년 1월 15일	

저자 유희태　**발행인** 박 용　**발행처** (주)박문각출판
표지디자인 박문각 디자인팀
등록 2015. 4. 29. 제2019-000137호
주소 06654 서울시 서초구 효령로 283 서경 B/D
팩스 (02) 584-2927
전화 교재 문의 (02) 6466-7202　동영상 문의 (02) 6466-7201

이 책의 무단 전재 또는 복제 행위는 저작권법 제136조에 의거, 5년 이하의 징역 또는 5,000만원 이하의 벌금에 처하거나 이를 병과할 수 있습니다.

정 가 39,000원(분권 포함)
ISBN 979-11-7519-462-5
ISBN 979-11-7519-461-8(세트)